Collins

English

English

GCSE Revision

English

Language & Literature

GCSE

Revision Guide

Paul Burns

English   Contents

Contents

	Revise	Practise	Review

Reading Task

Read the text below and answer the questions that follow.

> **From *Little Women* by Louisa May Alcott**
>
> 'Christmas won't be Christmas without any presents,' grumbled Jo, lying on the rug.
>
> 'It's so dreadful to be poor!' sighed Meg, looking down at her old dress.
>
> 'I don't think it's fair for some girls to have plenty of pretty things, and other girls nothing at all,' added little Amy, with an injured sniff.
>
> 'We've got Father and Mother, and each other,' said Beth contentedly from her corner.
>
> The four young faces on which the firelight shone brightened at the cheerful words, but darkened again as Jo said sadly, 'We haven't got Father, and shall not have him for a long time.' She didn't say perhaps never, but each silently added it, thinking of Father far away, where the fighting was.
>
> Nobody spoke for a minute; then Meg said in an altered tone, 'You know the reason Mother proposed not having any presents this Christmas was because it is going to be a hard winter for everyone; and she thinks we ought not to spend money for pleasure, when our men are suffering so in the army. We can't do much, but we can make our little sacrifices, and ought to do it gladly. But I am afraid I don't.' And Meg shook her head, as she thought regretfully of all the pretty things she wanted.
>
> 'But I don't think the little we should spend would do any good. We've each got a dollar, and the army wouldn't be much helped by our giving that. I agree not to expect anything from Mother or you, but I do want to buy *Undine and Sintram* for myself. I've wanted it so long,' said Jo, who was a bookworm.
>
> 'I planned to spend mine in new music,' said Beth, with a little sigh, which no one heard but the hearth brush and kettle holder.
>
> 'I shall get a nice box of Faber's drawing pencils. I really need them,' said Amy decidedly.

1 At the start of the extract which of the girls seems the happiest?

Support your answer with evidence from the text.

_____

_____ [3]

2 Why is the girls' father not living with them?

_____ [1]

3 **a)** What is it that the girls all think about their father but do not say?

_____

b) Why do you think they do not say it?

_____ [2]

4 What is meant by the following expressions?

a) Little sacrifices

_____

b) A bookworm

_____ [2]

5 Using your own words, explain Jo's argument for spending the money.

_____

_____ [2]

6 Why does the writer use the past tense ('I planned') when Beth is talking about what she would like, and the future ('I shall') when Amy speaks?

_____

_____ [3]

7 What do we learn about the characters and situation of the four girls?

Think about:
- the situation of the family as a whole
- how they behave and what they are interested in
- what they say and how they speak.

_____

_____

_____ [5]

Writing Task

Thank-You Letter

8 Your grandfather lives abroad and was not able to come home for your birthday. However, he sent you a present. Here is part of the letter that came with it. You now want to reply to him, thanking him for the present and telling him all about your birthday.

I decided to send you money because I don't really know what you like now and I want you to get something you really want. Please let me know what you decided to spend the money on – and send me one of those lovely letters full of news, that I so enjoy reading.

Looking forward to hearing from you,

Love, Grandad

Write your letter on a separate piece of paper. [20]

Spelling

You must be able to:

- Spell basic and regular words
- Spell complex and irregular words.

Spelling Rules

- A lot of English spelling is regular, meaning it follows rules or patterns. Here are some of the most useful rules.

'i' before 'e' except after 'c'

- achieve
- receive

Changing the 'y' to 'ie'

- Change the 'y' to 'ie' when adding 's' to a word ending in 'y'.
  - berry – berries
  - pity – pities

  but only if there is a **consonant** before the 'y'. If there is a **vowel** before the 'y', you just add 's'.
  - boy – boys
  - say – says
- Follow the same rule when you add 'ed'.
  - pity – pitied
  - play – played

- To form the **plural** of words that end in 'o', add 'es' (potatoes), except for words taken from Italian (pianos).
- If a word ends in 's' or a 'buzzing' or 'hissing' sound, add 'es' (glasses, dashes).
- You can also learn when to double a letter before 'ing' or 'ed'.
- Look for other patterns and rules that will help your spelling and learn them.

Homophones

- **Homophones** are words that sound the same but have different meanings. These cause a lot of problems. Here are some of the most common:
  - 'Here' means 'in this place': 'It's over here.'
  - You hear with your ears: 'I can hear you.'
  - 'There' means 'in that place': 'I put it over there.' It is also used in phrases such as 'there is' and 'there are'.
  - 'They're' is a **contraction** of 'they are': 'They're not really friends.'
  - 'Their' means 'belonging to them': 'They took all their things with them.'
  - 'Where', like 'here' and 'there', refers to place: 'Where do you think you're going?'

> ### Key Point
>
> Spelling matters: it helps you to make your meaning clear. You can – and should – work at improving your spelling.

- – 'Wear' is used about clothes etc.: 'You wear your earrings on your ears'.
- – 'We're and 'were' are not homophones but they often get mixed up:
  - * 'We're' is a contraction of 'we are': 'We're in the same class.'
  - * 'Were' is the **past tense** of 'are': 'We were very happy there.'
- – 'To' indicates direction: 'He went to the cinema.' It is also used as part of a **verb**: 'I want to do this now.'
- – 'Too' means excessively: 'Too much' or 'too many'.
- – 'Two' is the number 2: 'There were two questions to choose from.'

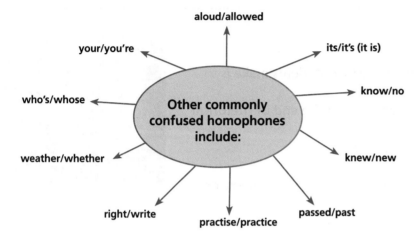

aloud/allowed

its/it's (it is)

your/you're

know/no

who's/whose

Other commonly confused homophones include:

knew/new

weather/whether

right/write

passed/past

practise/practice

Key Point

Identify the words you tend to get wrong. Make a list of them and set about learning them.

- • If you're not sure about any of these, look up their meanings and practise using them in sentences. You might be able to think of others that give you trouble.

Spelling Strategies

- • **Mnemonics** are ways of remembering things. It can be useful to learn a phrase where the first letters of the words spell out the word you are trying to spell:
  - – Big Elephants Can Always Upset Small Elephants (**because**).
- • Another useful trick is to **isolate** the part of the word that causes you trouble:
  - – There is **a rat** in sep**arat**e.
- • Or you might **associate** the spelling with the meaning of the word:
  - – **Necessary** – it is necessary to wear one collar, two socks
- • Some letters are not pronounced clearly, if at all (**silent letters**).
- • Try splitting up the word and saying it slowly and carefully to yourself:
  - – **en-vir-on-ment**
  - – **k-now-ledge**.

Key Words

consonant
vowel
plural
homophone
contraction
past tense
verb
mnemonic
isolate
associate
silent letter

Quick Test

Identify the correct spelling from the alternatives given in the following sentences:
1. We had know/no idea wear/where we were going.
2. Its/it's Monday today.
3. I can't decide weather/whether to/two/too buy it or not.
4. Hurry up or you'll miss football practice/practise.

Punctuation

You must be able to:

- Clearly demarcate sentences
- Accurately use a range of punctuation.

Ending Sentences

- Full stops separate sentences. A common mistake students make is to use commas instead of full stops.
- Question marks can be used in direct speech or at the end of rhetorical questions:
  - 'Do you really want to do that?' she asked.
  - Are we ready to meet the challenge?
- Exclamation marks are used to show surprise, shock and other extreme emotions:
  - What a monstrosity!
  - That's amazing!

Commas

- Commas are used to separate subordinate clauses from main clauses. Subordinate clauses give extra information but are not necessary for the sentence to make sense:
  - Mina, having run the marathon, was exhausted. ←
  - After eating two puddings, Ali was full. ←
- They are used in lists:
  - I ordered fish, chips, mushy peas and a fizzy drink.
- Commas are also used to introduce and to end direct speech:
  - He shouted, 'Leave me alone!'
  - 'Nobody move,' ordered the policeman.

'having run the marathon' is the subordinate clause

'After eating two puddings' is the subordinate clause

Colons and Semi-colons

- Colons are used before an explanation:
  - It took two hours: it was a difficult job.
- They introduce quotations:
  - Mercutio plays down his injury: 'Ay, ay, a scratch, a scratch.'
- They introduce lists:
  - The collection was wide and varied: historic manuscripts; suits of armour; ancient bones; and hundreds of old coins.
- Note that semi-colons are used to separate the items in the list above. Semi-colons separate items in a list that consist of more than one or two words. The semi-colon helps with clarity.
- Semi-colons are also used to show that two clauses are closely related, when the writer does not want to use a connective or a full stop:
  - The flowers are blooming; the trees are green.

> ### Key Point
>
> Commas must not be used to link clauses (statements which could stand alone as sentences) unless a connective or relative pronoun is used:
>
> I fed the cat, although it had already eaten.
>
> I fed the cat, which had already eaten.

Brackets, Dashes and Ellipsis

- Brackets (parentheses) go around a bit of extra information:
  - A huge man (he was at least seven feet tall) dashed across the road.
- Dashes can be used to show an interruption in the train of thought:
  - I finished the meal – if you could call it that – and quickly left.
- Ellipsis (…) indicates the omission of words from a sentence. It can be used to show a thought trailing off or to make the reader wonder what comes next:
  - I realized that I was not alone…

Inverted Commas

- Inverted commas can also be referred to as **speech marks** or **quotation marks**.
- Speech marks surround the actual words spoken:
  - 'Never again!' she cried.
- Similarly, when quoting from a text, you put the inverted commas (quotation marks) around any words taken from the original:
  - Tybalt refers to Romeo as 'that villain'.
- Inverted commas are also used for titles:
  - Shelley's 'Ozymandias' is about power.

Apostrophes

- **Apostrophes** are used to show **omission** (also called contraction), or **possession**.
- Only use apostrophes for omission when writing informally. In formal writing you should write all words in full. When you do use an apostrophe, put it where the missing letter or letters would have been:
  - You **shouldn't** have done that.
  - **Malik's** finished but **Rachel's** still working.
  - Let's go home.
- Apostrophes for possession show ownership. If the owner is singular, or a plural that does not end in 's', add an apostrophe and an 's' to the word that indicates the 'owner':
  - the cat's tail
  - the class's teacher
  - the children's toys
  - James's hat.
- The only time you have to do anything different is for a plural ending in 's'. In this case, simply add an apostrophe:
  - the cats' tails
  - the boys' team.

> ## Key Point
>
> Punctuation matters because writing does not make sense without it. Incorrect punctuation can change the meaning of your writing or even turn it into nonsense, confusing the reader.

> ## Key Words
>
> full stop
> comma
> question mark
> exclamation mark
> colon
> semi-colon
> parenthesis
> ellipsis
> inverted commas
> speech marks
> quotation marks
> apostrophe
> omission
> possession

> ## Quick Test
>
> Insert the correct punctuation:
> 1. Wheres my hamster Leo cried
> 2. He had gone there was no doubt about it
> 3. Maureen who lived next door searched her bins
> 4. Maureens son found Hammy in the kitchen

Sentence Structure

You must be able to:

- Use sentence structures accurately
- Use a variety of sentence structures for effect.

Simple Sentences

- Every sentence must contain a **subject** and a main **verb**. The subject is the person or thing (a **noun**) that the sentence is about. The verb is the doing, feeling or being word:

  Ronnie ate

  subject verb

- **Simple sentences** often include an **object** (also a noun).

  Ronnie ate an apple

  subject verb object

  'An apple' is the direct object. You can also use an indirect object:

  Ronnie ate at the table

  subject verb preposition object

  The **preposition** explains Ronnie's relationship to the table.

- You can vary simple sentences, and other sentence forms, by changing the verb from the **active** to the **passive voice**:

  The apple was eaten by Ronnie

  subject verb preposition agent

  Here the apple, by being put at the start of the sentence, becomes the subject.

Minor Sentences

- A minor sentence, also known as a **fragment**, is not really a sentence at all because it does not contain a main verb. These are very short and are used for effect. They are often answers to questions or exclamations:
  - Oh my word!
  - Just another boring day.
- They should be used rarely or they will lose their impact.

Compound Sentences

- To make a **compound sentence** you join together two **clauses** of equal importance using a **conjunction**. Clauses are phrases that could stand alone as simple sentences.
- You can use 'and', 'but' or 'or' to form compound sentences:
  - Lucia left the room and went to the shops.
  - Lucia left the room but stayed in the house.

> **Key Point**
>
> Try to vary the length and type of sentences you use. The examiner is looking for a range of sentence types being used.

- You can join more than two clauses in this way, though the result often appears clumsy:
  - Lucia left the room and went to the shops and bought a banana.

Complex Sentences

- A complex sentence also has two or more clauses joined together. The main clause should make sense on its own but the subordinate clause, which adds detail or explanation, does not need to.
- Some complex sentences are formed by joining two clauses with a conjunction. In these sentences the two clauses are not equal. Examples of conjunctions you might use are:

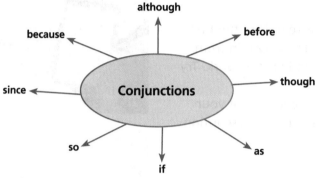

- The conjunction tells you what the relationship between the two clauses is:
  - Charlie left school **because** he had moved house.
  - Charlie left home **after** he had moved house.

  In the first sentence moving house is the reason for Charlie leaving school, whereas the second simply tells us the order in which the events happened.
- Sometimes the conjunction is placed at the beginning of the sentence rather than between the two clauses:
  - Although he felt ill, Dan ate an apple.
- Conjunctions are not needed to form complex sentences:
  - Maria, who loved shopping, left the house immediately.
  - Having left the house quickly, Maria went shopping.
- The first of these examples uses a relative pronoun (who) to connect the clauses, while the second changes the verb form to a past participle (having left).
- You can build even longer sentences by using several clauses and joining them in an appropriate way:
  - Dan was ill for several days so he stayed in bed, sometimes reading and sometimes watching television, but mostly bored and grumpy.

> **Key Point**
>
> Complex sentences can give more information and express more complex ideas.

> **Key Words**
>
> subject
> noun
> simple sentence
> object
> preposition
> active voice
> passive voice
> minor sentence
> fragment
> compound sentence
> clause
> conjunction
> complex sentence
> subordinate clause
> relative pronoun

> **Quick Test**
>
> Which of the following is (a) a simple sentence, (b) a compound sentence, (c) a complex sentence and (d) a minor sentence?
> 1. Never again.
> 2. The hamster was found safe and well.
> 3. She liked sheep but she hated cows.
> 4. Although she had been there before, the girl could not remember where she was.

Text Structure and Organization

You must be able to:

- Organize your writing in coherent paragraphs
- Use a range of discourse markers.

Paragraphs

- The traditional way of starting a new **paragraph** is to **indent** the first line of the new paragraph, that is, start a centimetre or two in from your margin. This is usual in most books, and in handwritten work. Try to do it in your exams.
- There is no set length for paragraphs. Try to vary the length of your paragraphs. You might use long paragraphs for a detailed description or explanation and short paragraphs for impact.

Starting a New Paragraph

> **Key Point**
>
> Paragraphs help you to organize your text so that it makes sense, follows a logical order and is easier to read.

- When you start writing about something new, you should start a new paragraph. This could be a change of:
  - **speaker** – when using direct speech, start a new paragraph when a new person speaks:

    'I didn't see anything,' added Marco.

  - **person** – introducing a new character:

    Julie was quite the opposite…

  - **place**:

    Toppington is also worth a visit…

  - **time**:

    A week later, Roland realized that all was not well…

  - **topic or idea** – moving from one aspect of your subject to another or introducing a different opinion:

    Another cause of concern is the local bus shelter…
    Some residents disagree with this view…

- Paragraphs often start with **topic sentences**, which introduce the topic or subject of the paragraph:

  When we left, there was nobody else on the boat.

  ← The topic of the paragraph is the boat and whether or not it was empty.

  Laurie Grantham, 17, has her own take on fashion.

  ← This paragraph is about Laurie's attitude to fashion.

Opening and Closing Paragraphs

- Opening and closing paragraphs can make a big difference to the impact of your writing. How you approach them depends on the form and purpose of your writing.
- Beginnings and endings in descriptive and narrative writing are dealt with on pages 40–43. Beginnings and endings in non-fiction are dealt with on page 30 and pages 49–51.

Discourse Markers

- **Discourse markers** connect sentences and paragraphs. They guide readers through the text, showing how one sentence relates to another and how one paragraph relates to another.
- They can be single-word **connectives**, such as 'however', or phrases, such as 'in addition to this'. A discourse marker can also be a phrase which picks up on an idea from the previous paragraph:
  - This kind of behaviour is common throughout Europe.
- Not all discourse markers (for example, 'however' and 'therefore') have to be used at the beginning of a sentence. They can be more effective a little way in.
- Discourse markers have many different purposes:

To add information or ideas	In addition; As well as; Furthermore; Moreover	The new building, moreover, will ruin the view from Huntington Hill.
To point out a similarity	Similarly; In the same way	Similarly, the owl hunts at night.
To introduce a contrasting idea or point of view	Nevertheless; On the other hand; In spite of; Alternatively	Some good points have been made in favour of the plan. Nevertheless, I still think it's a bad idea.
To express cause and effect	As a result; Consequently; In order to; Therefore	I have had no objections so far. I will, therefore, continue as planned.
To give order or to sum up	Firstly; Finally; In conclusion; Basically	Finally, I'd like to thank Josh for making all this possible.
To express passing time	Subsequently; Later; As soon as; Meanwhile	The police took an hour to arrive. Meanwhile, Archie had escaped.

> **Key Point**
>
> You do not have to use a discourse marker in every sentence or even every paragraph, especially in descriptive and narrative writing.

> **Quick Test**
>
> Identify the discourse markers in the following sentences and explain their purpose.
> 1. First, I will consider Ken's proposal.
> 2. Tom's idea, on the other hand, is ridiculous.
> 3. Before the bus shelter was built, there was no vandalism.
> 4. I suggest, therefore, that we demolish the bus shelter.

> **Key Words**
>
> paragraph
> indent
> topic sentence
> discourse marker
> connective

Standard English and Grammar

You must be able to:

- Use Standard English
- Use correct grammatical structures.

Standard English

- **Standard English** is the version of English that is widely accepted as being correct.
- You may not always have to write in Standard English. Characters in a story might use **dialect** or **slang**. If you are writing for teenagers or children, you might use the sort of language they would use with their friends.
- For all other purposes write in Standard English, using correct **grammar** and spelling.

Personal Pronouns: First Person

- The most common misuse of **personal pronouns** is the confusion of 'I' and 'me'. 'I' is the subject of the sentence; 'me' is the object:
  - 'Ikram and me were late' is clearly wrong because you would not say: 'Me was late.' You would say: 'I was late.' So, logically, it must be: 'Ikram and I were late.'
  - Similarly you should not say: 'They gave prizes to Lucy and I.' The correct form is: 'They gave prizes to Lucy and me.'

Personal Pronouns: Second Person

- 'You' is both the **singular** and **plural** form of the second person. You could say, 'Thank you for coming' to one person or to hundreds. There is no such word as 'yous'.
- Do not use the Americanism 'you guys'. 'Guys' is not Standard English.

Words and Phrases to Avoid

- Be aware of any words or phrases that are common in your area but are not Standard English, and avoid using them in formal writing.
- The same applies to current slang used by young people (such as 'sick' for 'good') and Americanisms, for example, using 'lay' instead of 'lie' or 'period' rather than 'full stop'.

> ### Key Point
>
> Standard English is the form of English which is most widely understood. You need to be able to use it so that your audience can understand what you are saying.

Modal Verbs

- Do not use the word 'of' instead of 'have' after **modal verbs** such as would, could, should and might:
  - If I'd known, I would **have** told you.

Verbs: Agreement and Tenses

- There are three basic tenses – past, **present** and future. This section focuses on the past tense because that is where most errors occur.
  - A common error is to confuse the first and **third person** of the verb, for example, using 'you was' instead of 'you were'.
  - Another is the confusion of the **simple past tense** and the **perfect tense**, which expresses a completed action (for example, using 'done' instead of 'did' or 'has done'). The perfect tense is formed by adding the past participle to 'have' or 'has'.
- Most verbs follow this pattern:

	Singular	Plural
Simple past	I/you/he/she/it walked.	We/you/they walked.
Perfect	I/you have walked. He/she/it has walked.	We/you/they have walked.

- Many of the most commonly used verbs are irregular, among them the verb 'to be'. These are its correct forms:

	Singular	Plural
Simple past	I was.	We were.
	You were.	You were.
	He/she/it was.	They were.
Perfect	I/you have been.	We/you have been.
	He/she/it has been.	They have been.

- Some other irregular verbs which cause problems are shown here.

Simple Past	Perfect	Simple Past	Perfect
ate	have/has eaten	sang	has/has sung
did	have/has done	saw	have/has seen
drove	have/has driven	spoke	have/has spoken
gave	have/has given	taught	have/has taught
got	have/has got	went	have/has gone
lay	have/has lain	woke	have/has woken

- If you are writing in the past tense and you want to refer to something that happened before the events you are describing, use the **past perfect tense**, which is formed using 'had' and the past participle:
  - She had eaten before she arrived.
- If you are writing about an event in the past which continued for some time, use the **past continuous**, formed by the past tense of the verb 'to be' and the present participle:
  - She was eating for the whole journey.

Key Words

Standard English
dialect
slang
grammar
personal pronoun
singular
plural
modal verb
present tense
third person
simple past tense
perfect tense
past perfect tense
past continuous tense

Quick Test

Rewrite the following sentences in Standard English:
1. Me and Jay was put on detention.
2. I seen you guys on Saturday.
3. You was the bestest player we had.
4. After we had sang the first number, we done a dance.

1 The following paragraph includes 10 incorrect spellings. Find them and rewrite them correctly.

> We where hoping for good whether for Sports Day. Unfortunately, on Friday morning it was poring with rain. Luckily, by ten o'clock it was clear and sunny. I was very exited when I got to the stadium but I had a long weight for my race, the 200 meters. Their were eight of us in the final. I was in the inside lane, witch I don't usually like, but I ran well round the bend and was second comming into the straight. As I crossed the line I was neck and neck with Jo. It wasn't until the teacher congratulated me that I knew I had definately won.

_____

_____ [10]

2 The following five sentences have been written without punctuation.
Insert the correct punctuation.

a) Peter Kowalski who was the tallest boy in the class easily won the high jump.

_____

b) What are you doing in the sand pit shouted Miss O'Connor get out of there at once.

_____

c) Francesca won medals for the long jump the high jump and the relay.

_____

d) I wasnt entered in any of the races because Im hopeless at running.

_____

e) Jonathan finished last however he was pleased with his time.

_____ [5]

3 **a)** Change each of the following pairs of sentences into single sentences, using conjunctions.

i) Julia stayed off school. She had a stomach ache.

_____

ii) He might be in the changing rooms. He might have already left.

_____

b) Change the following pairs of sentences into single sentences using relative pronouns.

i) Michael announced the results. He has a really loud voice.

_____

ii) The form with the best results won a cup. The cup was presented by Mr Cadogan.

_____

c) Turn the following three sentences into a single sentence.

    i) Maria had won the discus competition. She went home early. She was feeling sick.

_____ [5]

4 Rewrite the following sentences using Standard English.

a) Me and Hayley is going to town tomorrow.

_____

b) You guys can come wiv us if youse want.

_____

c) We was well chuffed with what we bought.

_____

d) I don't know nothing about what they done at school.

_____

e) I aint skiving off again coz I wanna get my GCSEs.

_____ [5]

5 Insert each of the following five connectives or discourse markers in the text below to help it to make sense.

however   **as well as**   **also**   **as a result of**   **consequently**

I am disgusted by the plan to close our library. (1)_____ having a massive impact on our community, this act of vandalism shows how little interest the council has in education. (2) _____ this attitude, our children are being deprived of a wonderful resource. Adults, especially older people, (3) _____ benefit greatly from the library. The council says we can use Hartington Library, but that is much too far away for most pensioners. (4) _____, they will lose what has become for many a real lifeline, making them feel part of the community. (5) _____, it does not have to be like this. There are other ways for the council to save money: we could start with cutting down on the Mayor's free trips to America!   [5]

6 Rewrite the following paragraph on a separate piece of paper, correcting errors in spelling, punctuation and grammar.

My first experiance of Bingley Park Library was when I was five. My grandmother, who were an avid reader, visitted the library every week and always borrowed four books. She read more or less anything but she especially liked detective story's, gardening books, and film star's biografies. Naturally, she wanted the rest of her family to be as enthusiastic as she was about books therefore, as soon as I could read, me and her marched down to bingley park. It was an imposing and rather frightening edifice for a child of five, the librarian, Miss Maloney, was just as imposing and twice as intimidating.   [10]

Explicit Information and Ideas

You must be able to:

- Identify and interpret explicit information and ideas.

Explicit Information

- **Explicit** information is information that is openly stated. You will find it in the text.
- It does not matter whether you think what the writer says is true or plausible. You are required to find the information and repeat it, either in the writer's words or in your own.
- Questions about explicit information could ask you to **identify** a piece of information or to list a number of pieces of information, for example:
  - How many species of butterfly are there?
  - List four things the writer tells you about butterflies.
- Read the text below and list four things the writer tells us about Griselda the cat:

> There were only two places where Griselda would sit in the garden: in the middle of the lawn (to catch the sun) and (if the sun was too hot) in the shade of the plum tree. She sometimes hunted at night and would return in the morning with little presents for us, mice or birds, which she always left in the middle of the kitchen floor to make sure we got them.

- You could say:
  - She would only sit in two places in the garden.
  - She liked to sit in the middle of the lawn.
  - If it was hot she sat under the plum tree.
  - She hunted at night.
  - She brought back mice and birds.
  - She left mice and birds in the kitchen.

  If the question asks for four facts you do not get marks for giving more than four.
- You would not get marks for:
  - She was a cat – you are told this in the question, not in the text.
  - She was friendly – there is no mention of this in the text.
  - There was a plum tree in the garden – true, but it is not about Griselda.

> **Key Point**
>
> You may be directed to a section of the text. Make sure you take your information only from that part of the text.

Explicit Ideas

- Explicit ideas are ideas and **opinions** that are openly stated.
- You could be asked, for example:
  - List four reasons given for the start of the war.
  - What does the writer think about the war?

- Explain why the writer's attitude to the war has changed.
- Which of the following, according to the writer, was not a cause of the war?

• Read the text below and explain how the writer thinks the park could be improved:

> Bilberry Recreation Ground is an eyesore. It is time for radical action. Let's start by getting rid of the graffiti – it's not art; it's vandalism. The Victorian benches are also in a sad state – let's restore them. There used to be beautiful flower beds. It's time we planted some new ones. Let's encourage families to return by building a new and exciting playground. What about a kiosk selling cups of tea and ice cream? Finally, may I suggest a change of name? 'Recreation Ground' sounds old-fashioned and dreary. Let's call it Bilberry Park from now on.

• You would get marks for mentioning the following points:
  - Get rid of the graffiti.
  - Restore the park benches.
  - Plant new flower beds.
  - Build a playground.
  - Build a refreshment kiosk.
  - Change the name.
• You would not get marks for:
  - It is an eyesore – this is not an idea for improvement.
  - Put a fence round the park – you might think this is a good idea but the writer does not mention it.
  - Take radical action – this is too vague.

Key Point

It does not matter whether you agree with what the writer says. You are being asked to identify the writer's ideas, not yours.

Quick Test

1. What does 'explicit' mean?
2. Can you quote from the text?
3. Can you put the answer in your own words?
4. If you are asked to list four points, do you get an extra mark for giving five?

Key Words

explicit
identify
opinion

Implicit Information and Ideas

You must be able to:

- Identify and interpret implicit information and ideas.

Implicit Information

- **Implicit** information is not stated openly. It is **implied**, so you have to 'read between the lines' to **infer** it from the text.
- Sometimes information is implied by saying what is not true:
  - He was not a happy child.
  This implies that he was sad.
- One piece of information can be implied by giving another:
  - They painted their garden shed blue.
  We can infer from this that they had a garden. Otherwise it would not be a 'garden' shed.

Implicit Ideas

- Similarly, writers can make their views and feelings clear without openly stating them:
  - I would rather stick pins in my eyes than sit through another maths lesson.
  This implies that the writer does not like maths.
- When you infer meaning and explain what you have inferred, you are **interpreting** implicit information or ideas.
- Sometimes we infer a writer's views or feelings by putting together a number of pieces of **evidence**. Read the following text:

> One thing that really annoys me is the way they constantly scratch themselves. And every dog I've ever met has had smelly breath. As for the constant barking and yapping! Give me a nice quiet cat or hamster any day.

Key Point

To imply something means to suggest something without expressly stating it. If you infer something you understand something which has been implied.

If you were asked whether the writer likes dogs, you could only answer 'no'. He or she does not ever say 'I don't like dogs', but gives three negative opinions about them and no positive ones.

True or False?

- Read the following passage:

I Left My Heart on Bilberry Rec

by Mary Goodenough

Bilberry Rec is a part of my past. It didn't have wonderful facilities or beautiful vistas. There were no rose gardens or tea shops, no adventure playgrounds and certainly no 'wild meadows'. There were a few trees and hedges, the 'swing park' and a football pitch.

It was what it said it was: a recreation ground, a place where people of all ages went for recreation. Small children played on the swings and didn't often bash their heads on the concrete floor. Bigger children played football or cricket – or just fought. Courting couples walked hand in hand along the muddy paths or snogged on the broken benches. Pensioners walked their dogs and everyone used it as a short cut.

I know times have changed. And my head tells me the new Bilberry Park will be much nicer (and cleaner and safer) than the old Rec, but my heart wants it left just as it is. It's a sure sign of getting older – an attack of illogical nostalgia.

- Which of the following statements are TRUE?
  1. Mary Goodenough has happy memories of Bilberry Rec.
  2. There was a rose garden in Bilberry Rec.
  3. The new park will have better facilities than the old Rec.
  4. Goodenough didn't feel safe in the Rec.
  5. Bilberry Rec was a beautiful place.
  6. Sometimes there were accidents in the swing park.
  7. Goodenough understands why things should change.
  8. Bilberry Rec is going to be built on.

- Numbers 1, 3, 6 and 7 are true.
  - 1 is implied by references to her 'heart' and nostalgia.
  - 3 is implied by referring to what the old Rec didn't have and calling the new park 'nicer...cleaner and safer'.
  - 6 is implied by saying that it didn't happen 'often'.
  - 7 is implied by saying that her 'head' tells her it will be better and that her nostalgia is 'illogical'.

> **Key Words**
>
> implicit
> imply
> infer
> interpret
> evidence

> **Quick Test**
>
> 1. Who implies, the writer or the reader?
> 2. Who infers?
> 3. Should you give your opinion?

Synthesis and Summary

You must be able to:

- Select and synthesize evidence from different texts
- Summarize the content of texts.

Synthesis

- Synthesis is the bringing together of parts to make a whole. In exams this usually takes the form of writing about two different texts.
- In your exam you may be asked to compare the **contents** of two texts.
- The texts will be about similar subjects but may have been written at different times, so it is likely that there will be differences in attitudes as well as in the things and people described.
- If you are asked to compare the contents of two texts, write about them both at equal length. Do not write about one and then the other. Write about both throughout your answer, discussing different aspects of the texts as you go.

Summary

- A summary is a shortened version of something, keeping the main points but leaving out unnecessary detail.
- When you write a summary do not add your own thoughts or comment on the writers' style or techniques.
- You should use evidence from the text in the form of short quotations but most of the answer should be in your own words. Do not copy out huge chunks of the text.

> **Key Point**
>
> Remember to look for both explicit and implicit information and ideas.

Approaching the Question

- **Read** the question carefully. It will have a particular focus, for example:
    - Write a summary of the differences between Mary and Jordan.
    - Summarize the different feelings of the writers about school.
  It might not use the words 'summary' or 'summarize' at all, for example:
    - What are the similarities and differences between Mary's and Jordan's experiences?
  Or you could be asked to compare contents as part of a longer question, for example:
- Both texts are about education. Compare the following:
    - the writers' feelings about their education
    - how they express these feelings.
- Skim read both texts.
- Underline or highlight the main points in the texts.
- You might want to do a (very quick) plan, listing differences and/or similarities.
- Focus on the question.
- Don't repeat yourself.

- Don't waste time on an introductory and concluding paragraph.
- Write in proper sentences and paragraphs, using connectives.

Example
- Below are two short extracts from texts about sea voyages. Think about what you would include if you were asked to write about the differences between the voyages:

> ### Daily Southern Cross, 21 October 1859
>
> The *Mermaid* […] arrived in harbour on Wednesday at 4 a.m. She left Liverpool on 11th July at 5 p.m. Passengers have been very healthy during the voyage; three infants died, and one birth occurred. The passengers speak highly of Captain White and officers.

> ### The Northern Star, 21 October 2014
>
> After three weeks the luxury liner *Ariadne* finally arrived home and the passengers disembarked from the journey one of them described as 'a floating nightmare'. For the last week almost a quarter of the passengers had been confined to their cabins with mild food poisoning and many are now demanding their money back.

- You could pick out the following differences:

Mermaid	Ariadne
Journey over three months	Three-week journey
Passengers 'healthy' – three infants died	Food poisoning
Passengers praise captain and crew	Passengers demand money back

- A paragraph about the differences might read:

> *The Mermaid's journey lasted over three months; Ariadne's took three weeks. The Mermaid's passengers are 'healthy' but the Ariadne's have food poisoning. However, 'three infants died' on the Mermaid, suggesting that not everyone was healthy. Nevertheless, it would seem that the Victorian passengers were happier than the modern ones, as they 'speak highly' of the crew rather than complaining.*

Quick Test

1. Should the summary be shorter than the original text?
2. Should you use quotations in your summary?
3. Should you discuss the writers' use of language in your answer?

Referring to the Text

You must be able to:

- Select appropriate and relevant examples from texts
- Use textual references to support and illustrate your interpretation of the texts.

Referring to the Text

- You can **refer** to a text by **paraphrasing** the text or by **quoting** from the text.
- For all Language questions and some Literature questions, you will have a text in front of you from which you can take your examples.
- For other Literature questions you will have to rely on your memory, so it is a good idea to learn some significant quotations.

Paraphrasing

- Paraphrasing means putting something into your own words. It is useful for summing up, for example:

> *The writer gives us a number of examples of cruelty to animals such as neglect and physical violence, which he describes in very vivid terms.*

- When you are writing about a longer text, such as a novel, you might not need to quote because you are writing about events or feelings and the exact wording is not important:

> *Lydia clearly does not think much about her family's reputation. When she returns from London she does not express any shame at her behaviour but boasts about being married.*

> **Key Point**
>
> It is very important to refer to the text in your answers, both in English Language and English Literature exams.

Using Quotations

- A **quotation** is a word or phrase taken directly from the text. Indicate that you are quoting by putting inverted commas (or quotation marks) around the quotation.
- There are three main ways to set out your quotations.
- If your quotation consists of just a few words (or even one word) and fits naturally into your sentence, you simply put it into inverted commas (quotation marks):

> *At the start of the soliloquy Juliet refers to 'love-performing night' but later it becomes a 'sober suited matron all in black'.*

This is called **embedding**. Examiners like you to embed and it should be the method you use most often.

- If the quotation will not fit easily into your sentence but is fairly short (no more than 40 words of prose or one line of verse), put a colon (:) before it, continue on the same line and use inverted commas:

> Benvolio passionately asserts that he is not lying: 'This is the truth or let Benvolio die.'

- If you want to use a longer quotation, leave a line and indent. You must indent the whole quotation. When quoting verse, end the lines where they end in the original. Do not use inverted commas:

> This opposition will inevitably cause problems for the lovers and Juliet expresses her dilemma:
>
> > My only love sprung from my only hate!
> > Too early seen unknown and known too late!
>
> The use of paradox emphasizes her confusion.

Using PEE

- Remember to use PEE (Point, Evidence, Explanation).
- First make your **point**, saying what you want to say about the text.
- Then give your **evidence**, either in the form of a paraphrase or a quotation.
- Finally, **explain** or explore the evidence you have given.

> The writer is very concerned about what he sees as widespread cruelty to domestic animals. He mentions the 'heartless neglect' of some dogs by their owners. The use of this emotive adjective paints the owners as villains and appeals to the compassion of the readers.

Here the first sentence makes the point, the second gives the evidence in quotation marks, and the third explains/explores the evidence.

Analysing Language 1

You must be able to:

- Explain, comment on and analyse how writers use language
- Use relevant subject terminology to support your views.

Diction and Register

- **Diction** and **register** both refer to the writer's choice of words or vocabulary.
- Most texts you read will be in Standard English. Sometimes, however, you will come across a text that uses a lot of non-standard words, for example slang and dialect words (see pages 14–15).
- Their use can tell you something about the writer, the narrator, certain characters or the audience at which the text is aimed.
- Writers might use specialized diction: for example, a lot of scientific or medical terms. The use of such language shows that the text is aimed at people who are interested in the subject and probably already know quite a lot about it.
- Writers might use words and expressions associated with a particular subject – for example, war or nature – for rhetorical or figurative purposes. Sometimes their word choice is referred to as a **semantic field**. We can often infer their attitude to the subject from their choice of semantic field.

Parts of Speech (Word Classes)

- **Nouns** are naming words.
  - **Concrete nouns** name objects (chair, mountain).
  - **Abstract nouns** name ideas and feelings (love, suspicion).
  - **Proper nouns** have capital letters and name individual people (Jelena), places (Warsaw), days of the week (Saturday), months (April) etc.
  - A 'noun phrase' is a group of words built around a noun.
- **Adjectives** describe nouns (the **red** house; his **undying** love).
- **Verbs** are doing, feeling and being words. You might comment on whether verbs are:
  - in the past tense (she walked; he was thinking)
  - in the present tense (she is walking; he thinks)
  - or in the future tense (we are going to walk; you will go).
- **Adverbs** describe verbs, telling us how something is being done, for example, she spoke **slowly**; he writes **carefully**.
- **Pronouns** stand in for other words, usually nouns. Whether the writer uses first person (I/we), second person (you) or third person (he/she/ they) can make a difference to how we read the text. 'I' makes the text more personal to the writer. 'We' and 'you' aim to involve the reader more in the text. There are different types of pronouns.

> ### Key Point
>
> When we talk about 'parts of speech' or 'word class' we are referring to what words do in sentences. It is important that you can identify these so that you can refer easily to them in a way that shows you understand their function: for example, 'The writer uses a lot of adjectives associated with war to describe the scene.'

Personal pronouns	Relative pronouns
I/me	who
we/us	whom
you	whose
he/him	that
she/her	which
it	
they/them	

- **Prepositions** are used to express the relationship between nouns (or noun phrases) and other parts of the sentence or clause:
  - We went **to** the cinema.
  - The cat is **under** the table.
- **Conjunctions** join words, phrases and clauses: for example, 'and', 'but', 'although', 'because'. A conjunction is a type of connective but the two words are not interchangeable. Other types of word and phrase, including relative pronouns and adverbs, can also act as connectives (see Sentence Structure, pages 10–11).
- **Determiners** come before nouns and help to define them. The most common are the definite article (the) and the indefinite article (a/an). Other examples of determiners are 'this', 'both' and 'some'.

Key Words

diction
register
vocabulary
semantic field
noun
concrete noun
abstract noun
proper noun
adjective
verb
adverb
pronoun
preposition
conjunction
determiner

Quick Test

Read this sentence:
The old horse was munching thoughtfully on his oats.
Identify:
1. Two nouns
2. A verb
3. An adjective
4. A preposition
5. An adverb

Analysing Language 2

You must be able to:

- Explain, comment on and analyse how writers use language
- Use relevant subject terminology to support your views.

Connotation

- A **connotation** is an implied meaning. Words can have associations other than their literal meanings. For example, red indicates danger or anger. 'Heart' has connotations of love and sincerity.

> **Key Point**
>
> Writers use language to affect and influence their readers.

Emotive Language

- Writers often seek to arouse certain feelings or emotions in the reader, for example, pity or anger. This can be done by using **emotive language**: words and phrases that have certain connotations.
- A reporter writing about a crime could write:

> Burglars stole some jewellery from Mr Bolton's house.

This just tells us the facts. A writer who wanted to influence our emotions might write:

> Heartless burglars stole jewellery of great sentimental value from frail pensioner Albert Bolton.

The adjective 'heartless' makes the burglars sound deliberately cruel, and 'frail' emphasizes the weakness of the victim, while the phrase 'of great sentimental value' tells us how important the jewellery was to Mr Bolton. This increases our sympathy for him.

Rhetorical Language

- **Rhetoric** is the art of speaking. Effective speakers have developed ways of influencing their audiences. Writers also use rhetorical techniques to affect readers.
- **Hyperbole** is another word for exaggeration:

> Councillor Williams is the most obnoxious man ever to disgrace this council chamber.

- **Lists of three** are used to hammer home a point:

> Friends, Romans, countrymen.

- **Repetition** is used to emphasize the importance of the point being made:

> Victory at all costs, victory in spite of all terror, victory however long and hard the road may be; for without victory there is no survival.

- **Rhetorical questions** are questions which do not need an answer. Sometimes the writer gives an answer:

> Can we do this? Yes, we can.

Sometimes they are left unanswered to make the reader think about the answer:

> What kind of people do they think we are?

Sound

- The sound of words can make a difference to their meaning and effect.
- **Onomatopoeia** is the use of words which sound like their meaning:

> The door creaked open and clunked shut.

- **Alliteration**, the use of a series of words starting with the same sound, is common in newspaper headlines as well as in poetry and other literary texts:
  - Brave Bella battles burglars.
  - Storm'd at with shot and shell.
- When you see alliteration, think about why the writer uses a particular sound. Some consonants ('d', 'k', 'g') are hard. Others ('s', 'f') are soft. 'P' and 'b' have an explosive quality.
- The repetition of 's' sounds is also referred to as **sibilance**.
- **Assonance** is the use of a series of similar vowel sounds for effect:

> From the bronzey soft sky…Tipples over and spills down.

Imagery

- Literal **imagery** is the use of description to convey a mood or atmosphere. A description of a storm might create an atmosphere of violence and danger.
- Figurative imagery uses an image of one thing to tell us about another.
  - **Similes** compare one thing to another directly, using 'like' or 'as':

  > Straight and slight as a young larch tree.

  - **Metaphors** imply a comparison. Something is written about *as if it were* something else:

  > Beth was a real angel.

  - **Personification** makes a thing, idea or feeling into a person:

  > At my back I always hear
  > Time's winged chariot hurrying near.

  - The personification of nature, giving it human qualities, is also called **pathetic fallacy**:

  > The clouds wept with joy.

  This term can also be applied to a literal description in which nature or the weather reflects the feelings of characters.
  - A **symbol** is an object which represents a feeling or idea, for example a dove to represent peace.

> **Key Point**
>
> Imagery is usually associated with literary texts, such as poems. However, non-fiction texts also use imagery to paint pictures in the readers' minds.

> **Key Words**
>
> connotation
> emotive language
> rhetoric
> hyperbole
> repetition
> rhetorical question
> onomatopoeia
> alliteration
> sibilance
> assonance
> imagery
> simile
> metaphor
> personification
> pathetic fallacy
> symbol

Quick Test

Of which literary techniques are the following examples?
1. Macbeth doth murder sleep.
2. Ill met by moonlight.
3. I wandered lonely as a cloud.
4. You were sunrise to me.

Analysing Form and Structure

You must be able to:

- Explain, comment on and analyse how writers use form and structure
- Use relevant subject terminology to support your views.

Form and Structure

- The structure of a text is the way in which it is organized: for example, the order in which information is given or events described.
- The terms 'structure' and 'form' are both used to describe how a text is set out on the page.

Openings

- The beginning (opening) of a text is very important as it has to draw in the readers and encourage them to continue reading.
- Some texts begin by giving an overview of the subject, indicating what the text is going to be about:

> There are thousands of varieties of butterfly. In this article I will discuss some of the most common.

- A writer might explain why he or she has decided to write:

> Lewis's views about youth unemployment are fundamentally wrong.

- Fiction writers can use their openings to introduce characters or settings:

> 'I shall never forget Tony's face,' said the carrier.

- Texts can also start with dramatic statements, designed to shock, surprise or intrigue:

> It was a bright cold day in April, and the clocks were striking thirteen.

Endings

- Fiction writers might give a neat conclusion: for example, with the solving of a crime or a marriage:

> Reader, I married him.

- They might prefer to leave us with a sense of mystery or suspense:

> 'Who are they?' asked George […]
> 'Wolves.'

- Writers of essays and articles usually end by drawing together their main points and reaching a conclusion.
- Some texts end with a question or even an instruction:

> Get out there now and use your vote!

> **Key Point**
>
> You should consider why the writer has decided to arrange things in a particular way and the effect of this on the reader.

Chronological Order

- **Chronological order** gives events in the order in which they happened. This is the most common way of ordering fiction, and non-fiction texts such as histories, biographies and travel writing.
- Writers might, however, start at the end of the story or somewhere in the middle before going back to recap previous events in 'flashbacks'.
- **Reverse chronological order** means starting with the latest event and working backwards. You will see this in **blogs** and discussion forums.

Other Ways of Ordering Texts

- Some texts start with general information and move on to more detailed information and explanation.
- A text giving a point of view might build up to what the writer thinks are the most persuasive arguments.
- Information can be arranged in **alphabetical order**, as in dictionaries and encyclopaedias.
- Texts sometimes rank things or people in order of importance or popularity, as in a music chart, either starting with the best and working down or starting with the worst and working up.

Divisions

- Books are usually divided into **chapters**, sometimes with titles or numbers.
- Most prose is arranged in **paragraphs** (see pages 12–13), while verse is often divided into **stanzas** (see pages 98–99). Make sure you use the correct terminology.
- Other devices used to divide up text include **bullet points**, numbering and **text boxes**. Headlines and subheadings help to guide readers through the text.

Analysing Structure

- When analysing a short text, or an extract from a longer text, think about how and why the writer changes focus from one paragraph or section to another, perhaps moving from a general description to something more detailed, from a group of people to a particular character, or from description to action or speech.

> **Key Point**
>
> Texts, especially longer texts, are often divided into sections. These give order to their contents and help readers find their way through the text.

> **Key Words**
>
> opening
> conclusion
> chronological order
> reverse chronological order
> blog
> alphabetical order
> chapter
> paragraph
> stanza
> bullet point
> text box

> **Quick Test**
>
> Put the following in:
> 1. chronological order
> 2. reverse chronological order
> 3. alphabetical order
>   a) December 2014
>   b) January 2002
>   c) April 2011
>   d) November 2011

1 Insert the correctly spelled word in each of the following pairs of sentences.

    a) except/accept

        I did them all _____ the last one.

        I _____ your apology.

    b) affect/effect

        The weather seemed to have a bad _____ on everyone's mood.

        I don't think the weather will _____ the result.

    c) aloud/allowed

        Nobody is _____ in here at lunchtime.

        Mo really likes reading _____ in class.

    d) write/right

        Nobody got the _____ answer.

        I'll _____ a letter and explain.

    e) who's/whose

        He couldn't return it because he didn't know _____ coat it was.

        Tell me _____ going and then I'll decide.   **[5]**

2 Rewrite the following passage on a separate piece of paper using the correct punctuation.

> dont you think we should wait for him asked Eve
>
> not at all Henry replied he never waits for us
>
> well that's true Eve replied but he doesn't know the way

    [10]

3 Rewrite the following passage on a separate piece of paper, using a variety of simple, compound and complex sentences (and adding words if necessary) to make it more effective. **[10]**

> Henry and Eve waited for another ten minutes. Joel did not arrive. They left without him. They walked to the bus stop. There was no-one there. This suggested they had just missed the bus. Henry was very annoyed with Joel. Eve told him to calm down. She told him to forget about Joel. The journey was uneventful. They got off the bus by the lake. It looked eerie in the moonlight. They sat down on a grassy bank. They took their sandwiches and drinks out of the bag. Henry felt a hand on his shoulder.

    [10]

4 Pick the five sentences in which the correct forms of the verb are used.

    a) You was really good tonight.   ☐

    b) Ms Greenall taught me how to boil an egg.   ☐

c) They've gotten two more kittens. ☐

d) I knew the song because we had sung it in class. ☐

e) I rung the bell twice but nobody come. ☐

f) She lay on the sofa until she felt better. ☐

g) I done my homework at break. ☐

h) He says he won't come because he's already seen it. ☐

i) I have done what you asked. ☐

j) I'm going to lay down here for a while. ☐ [5]

5 Put the following nouns into their plural forms.

a) pizza _____

b) latch _____

c) mosquito _____

d) sheep _____

e) donkey _____

f) stadium _____

g) quality _____

h) church _____

i) woman _____

j) hypothesis _____ [5]

6 Rearrange the following paragraphs so that the whole letter makes sense.

a) The next thing I knew two young girls were leaning over me. I'm sorry to say I thought the worst when I saw the rings through their noses. But they asked me if I was all right and very gently helped me to stand up. One of them stayed with me while the other went into the shop and fetched a chair. Then I noticed there were two boys carefully collecting all my shopping and bagging it up.

b) When it was all collected in, they called a taxi to take me home. I'm sorry to say I didn't ask their names, so I'd like to give them a big thank you through your newspaper. Whoever you are, you're a real credit to Bilberry and to your generation!

c) I was in town on Wednesday to do my usual shop in the supermarket. I got a little more than usual so my bags were rather heavy. As I came out of the shop I lost my balance and keeled over, spilling all my shopping.

d) I wasn't badly hurt but it was quite a shock. I just sat there on the pavement, stunned and not knowing what to do.

e) I am writing to express my thanks to a group of young people I met last week. It isn't often we hear good things about teenagers. We read so much about crime and vandalism, drinking and bad manners that we can easily end up thinking the worst of all teenagers.

a) ☐ **b)** ☐ **c)** ☐ **d)** ☐ **e)** ☐ [5]

Read the passage below.

From *A Christmas Carol* by Charles Dickens

Nobody ever stopped him in the street to say, with gladsome looks, 'My dear Scrooge, how are you? When will you come to see me?' No beggars implored him to bestow a trifle;[1] no children asked him what it was o'clock; no man or woman ever once in all his life inquired the way to such and such a place, of Scrooge. Even the blindmen's dogs appeared to know him; and when they saw him coming on, would tug their owners into doorways and up courts; and then would wag their tails as though they said, 'No eye at all is better than an evil eye, dark master!'

[1] *bestow a trifle* – to give a small amount

1 Find four ways in which other people react when they meet Scrooge.

_____

_____

_____

_____ [4]

2 How does Dickens use language to give us an impression of Scrooge's character? You could comment on his use of:
  - words and phrases
  - language feature and techniques
  - sentence forms.

Write your answer on a separate piece of paper. [8]

3 Read the passage below.

From a letter written by Charles Lamb to William Wordsworth

London, January 30, 1801

I ought before this to have replied to your very kind invitation into Cumberland. With you and your sister I could gang[1] anywhere. But I am afraid whether I shall ever be able to afford so desperate a Journey. Separate from the pleasure of your company, I don't much care if I never see a mountain in my life. I have passed all my days in London [...] The lighted shops of the Strand and Fleet Street, the innumerable trades, tradesmen and customers, coaches, waggons, playhouses, all the bustle and wickedness round about Covent Garden, the very women of the Town, the Watchmen, drunken scenes, rattles;[2]—life awake, if you awake, at all hours of the night, the impossibility of being dull in Fleet Street, the crowds, the very dirt & mud, the Sun shining upon houses and pavements, the print shops, the old *Book* stalls, [...] coffee houses, steams of soup from kitchens, the pantomimes, London itself a pantomime and a masquerade, all these things work themselves into my mind and feed me without a power of satiating me. The wonder of these sights impels me into night walks about the crowded streets, and I often shed tears in the motley Strand from fullness of joy at so much *Life*.— All these emotions must be strange to you. So are your rural emotions to me [...]

My attachments are all local, purely local.—I have no passion [...] to groves and valleys.—The rooms where I was born, the furniture which has been before my eyes all my life, a book case which has followed me about (like a faithful dog, only exceeding him in knowledge) wherever I have moved, old tables, streets, squares, where I have sunned myself, my old school,—these are my mistresses. Have I not enough, without your mountains?

[1] *gang* – a dialect word for 'go'
[2] *rattles* – constant chatterers

Look at lines 1–7.

a) Identify two phrases which show Lamb's feelings about Wordsworth.

_____ [2]

b) What do these phrases show about their relationship?

_____ [2]

4 Look at the whole of the extract. Which **three** of the following statements are TRUE?

a) Charles Lamb hates London. ☐

b) He has always lived in London. ☐

c) He finds life in the city exciting. ☐

d) He does not like going out after dark. ☐

e) He thinks Wordsworth will find it strange that he does not like the countryside. ☐

f) He loves climbing mountains. ☐ [3]

5 Now read this article and explain the differences between Weston's and Lamb's attitudes to city life. [8]

I'm a City-Hater – Get Me out of Here!

by Malcolm Weston

I've had enough. I'm leaving. Who was it who said that when a man is tired of London he's tired of life? Well, I don't think I'm tired of life – I'd like to go on living as long as I can – but I'm fed up to the back teeth with London. It's dirty. It's noisy. You can barely move in Oxford Street sometimes. Everything's expensive (how can anyone afford to live here?) And everyone is so bad-tempered. I know it's meant to be terribly lively and exciting but, frankly, I'm bored with it. Sorry, Londoners. It's nothing personal: I don't really like any cities – or towns. So I'm off home. And this time next week you'll find me (if you can – it's a bit off the beaten track) halfway up a mountain somewhere in the Lake District, looking up at the sky and listening to the sound of silence.

_____

_____

_____

_____

_____

_____

_____

_____

Reading Literary Texts 1

You must be able to:

- Read and understand a range of literature
- Critically evaluate literary texts.

Story Structure

- Most novels and stories begin by 'setting the scene', introducing characters or places and giving us a sense of the world we are entering.
- That world might be very like our own world but it could be unfamiliar, perhaps because the story is set in a different country or a different time.
- The writer might even, like Tolkien, have invented a complete fantasy world.
- This part of a story is called **exposition** and can take a chapter or more, or maybe just a few lines.
- The event that really gets the story going is sometimes called the **inciting incident**. This can be dramatic and shocking, like Pip's encounter with the convict at the beginning of *Great Expectations*, or it can be a seemingly ordinary event, like Darcy coming to stay with Bingley in *Pride and Prejudice*.
- Inciting incidents change the lives of the protagonists (the main characters) for ever.

Key Point

Every story has a beginning, a middle and an end. The extracts you will be given might come from any part of the story.

- During the course of a story there are usually several **turning points**. These are events which change the direction of the story for good or ill. Sometimes we can see them coming; sometimes they are unexpected and surprising 'twists' in the plot.
- Towards the end, most stories reach a **climax**, or denouement, when things come to a conclusion, sometimes happily as in a fairy tale, sometimes not. This is the event the whole story has been building up to.
- The climax is not always the end of the story. Most writers take some time to reflect on how things have turned out.
- Endings quite often refer back to openings, giving a sense of how things have changed.

Key Point

When analysing a literary text, always consider the 'narrative voice' and your reaction to it.

Narrative Perspectives

- Many stories are told in the first person singular ('I'), so that we see the story through the eyes of one of the characters, usually the **protagonist**, for example, Jane in *Jane Eyre* or Harri in *Pigeon English*. This encourages us to empathize with them.
- Sometimes the **narrator** is another character, acting more as an observer and putting some distance between the reader and the protagonist. Dr Watson in the Sherlock Holmes stories is an example of this.
- Each narrator has his or her own 'voice'. In *Pigeon English*, for example, the kind of language the narrator uses tells us about his background and culture.
- A writer might use different several narrators so that we get different characters' experiences and points of view: Mary Shelley does this in *Frankenstein*.
- In a 'third-person **narrative**' the narrator is not involved in the story at all. If there is a sense of the narrator's 'voice', it is the voice of the author. This gives the writer the opportunity of sharing with us the thoughts, feelings and experiences of many characters.
- A narrator who can see everything in this way is called an **omniscient narrator**.
- Sometimes omniscient narrators comment on characters and action using the first person. If so they are called **intrusive**. Dickens uses this technique in *A Christmas Carol*.

Key Words

exposition
inciting incident
turning point
climax
protagonist
narrator
narrative
omniscient narrator
intrusive narrator

Quick Test

1. Does the exposition come at the beginning or end?
2. When the narrator is part of the action is it a first-person or third-person narrative?
3. Which comes first: the climax or the inciting incident?
4. What is an omniscient narrator?

Reading Literary Texts 2

You must be able to:

- Read and understand a range of literature
- Critically evaluate texts.

Character

- We learn about **characters** in different ways.
- The narrator can directly describe a character. In this example (from *The Strange Case of Dr Jekyll and Mr Hyde*) we can infer something about the man's character from his appearance.

> …the lawyer was a man of a rugged countenance, that was never lighted by a smile.

> **Key Point**
>
> Descriptions of people make the characters seem more real and can tell us a lot about them.

- We can learn about characters from what they say and how they say it, as well as from what other characters say about and to them. In this quotation from *Pride and Prejudice* Mr Bennet gives his opinion of his daughters:

> 'They are all silly and ignorant like other girls; but Lizzy has something more of quickness than her sisters.'

We can infer from this that Lizzy is the only daughter that Mr Bennet is interested in and that he can be quite blunt and dismissive. However, we might get a slightly different impression if we know that he is talking to his wife. It could be that he is trying to provoke her and/or that his remark about the girls being 'silly and ignorant' is intended as a joke.

- Most importantly, you should consider how characters behave and how others react to them. Dickens leaves us in no doubt about Scrooge's character:

> Even the blindmen's dogs appeared to know him; and when they saw him coming on, would tug their owners into doorways and up courts.

This comes at the beginning of *A Christmas Carol* and gives us a strong first impression, which is built on by descriptions of his treatment of his clerk, his nephew and the men who come collecting for charity.

Description

- This description (from *The Withered Arm* by Thomas Hardy) is fairly simple:

  > …it was not a main road; and the long white riband of gravel that stretched before them was empty, save for one moving speck.

  This tells us that the story is set in a remote place and sets up the encounter between the people in the carriage and the boy, whom they first see as a 'moving speck'.

- In the first chapter of *Great Expectations*, Dickens describes the **setting** in a way that gives us information about the landscape while creating an **atmosphere** that prepares us for the frightening event that is about to happen:

  > …and that the dark flat wilderness beyond the churchyard, intersected with dykes and mounds and gates, with scattered cattle feeding on it, was the marshes; and that the low leaden line beyond, was the river; and that the distant savage lair from which the wind was rushing, was the sea…

  Dickens uses adjectives like 'dark', 'low' and 'leaden' to give us a sense of an unattractive, featureless landscape, but adds words like 'wilderness' and 'savage' to make it seem dangerous and threatening.

- The description above uses **literal imagery** to create **mood** and atmosphere, the lonely, rather frightening place reflecting the feelings of the protagonist Pip.
- **Figurative imagery**, too, is often used in descriptive writing. In *The Withered Arm* Hardy uses a simile to describe one of his characters:

  > Her face too was fresh in colour, but it was of a totally different quality – soft and evanescent, like the light under a heap of rose-petals.

  The imagery helps us to picture her complexion and gives us a sense of her beauty and fragility.

Key Point

Writers describe places to root their stories in a time and place, and to create mood and atmosphere.

Quick Test

Identify what kind of imagery is being used in these sentences:
1. The lake shone like a silver mirror.
2. Angry crags surrounded us.
3. A veil of snow hid it from view.
4. There was a cluster of jagged black rocks.

Key Words

character
setting
atmosphere
literal imagery
mood
figurative imagery

Narrative Writing

You must be able to:

- Write clear and imaginative narratives.

Narrative

- A narrative is an account of events – a story, whether real or imagined.
- In your exam you may be asked to write a story or part of a story. This gives you the opportunity to use your imagination and be creative.
- You may be asked to write for a particular audience. If so, it is most likely to be for people of your own age.
- You will be given a 'stimulus' for your story. This could be a picture or just a brief instruction:
  - Write the opening of a story suggested by the picture above.
  - Write about someone whose life changes suddenly.
  These instructions are often deliberately vague, so you can develop your own ideas in your own style.

Planning

- Before you start to write, spend a few minutes planning, making decisions about the main elements of your story.

Character and Voice

- Decide whether you are going to write in the first or third person. If you opt for the first person, is the narrator the protagonist or an observer?

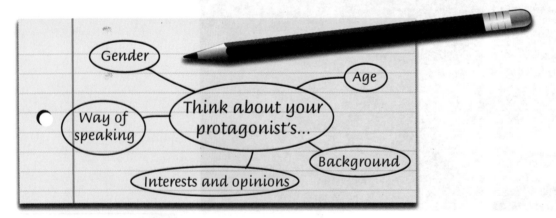

- The protagonist could be you or a version of you, but it can be much more interesting to write about someone who is completely different.
- There may also be an antagonist, someone who stands in the way of or opposes the protagonist.
- Think about other, minor characters – but beware of inventing too many. You don't want to make things too complicated.

> **Key Point**
>
> You can tell a story in your own voice or you can invent a character (persona) to tell the story.

Structure

- The same applies to the plot. If you are writing a complete story, keep it fairly simple.
  - You need an inciting incident, a climax and at least one turning point, but not too many.
  - You need to establish your 'world,' but don't spend too much time on exposition.
  - You might end with a shock or surprise. It has been said that writers should give their readers what they want but not in the way they expect.
- If you are only writing the opening, make sure something interesting or dramatic happens that would make a reader want to know what happens in the rest of the story. You should know how the story would develop and end.
- It is less likely that you would be asked to write the end of a story, but if you are asked to do this, you need to know what happened before the point at which you start your story.
- Stories are normally written mainly in chronological order but you might want to use 'flashbacks'.

Language and Style

- Normally you would write in Standard English but if you use a first-person narrator, you should write in that person's voice. Think about its tone – formal or chatty? – as well as whether to use dialect or slang.
- Stories, whether true or imagined, are usually written in the past tense. Using the present tense can make the action seem more immediate and vivid, though. You can use either, but stick to one.
- Direct speech can help to move on the story and tell us about character, but use it sparingly. Think about whether it adds anything – and make sure you set it out properly. Sometimes indirect (or reported) speech can be more effective.
- Write in paragraphs. These should usually be linked by discourse markers, particularly ones that relate to time:
  - After they left, he sank to his knees.
- Use a variety of sentence structures, for example using complex sentences for descriptions and simple or even minor sentences for dramatic impact:
  - It was her.
  - A gun beneath the leaves.
- Use a range of punctuation but avoid using a lot of exclamation marks.

Key Point

Be careful not to just tell the 'bare bones' of the story. You also need to describe people and places.

Quick Test

What is meant by the following?
1. The protagonist.
2. The antagonist.
3. The inciting incident.
4. A turning point.

Key Words

narrative
protagonist
antagonist
voice
direct speech
indirect speech
reported speech

Descriptive Writing

You must be able to:

- Write clear and imaginative descriptions.

Description

- One of the tasks in your exam could be to write a description, possibly based on a picture or pictures. If there is a picture, you are not limited to describing what is actually in the picture. It is there to stimulate your imagination.
- When writing a description you can draw on your memories of real people, places or things.
- You might also be inspired by something you've read.
- Think about different aspects of your subject – and not just positive ones. This is especially important when describing a person – there is only so much you can write about how lovely someone is.
- Think about all five senses: sight, hearing, smell, taste and touch. When you have decided what you want to describe, it is a good idea to jot down what you experience through each sense. If you were describing a beach you might put:

Taste	Touch	Hearing	Smell	Sight
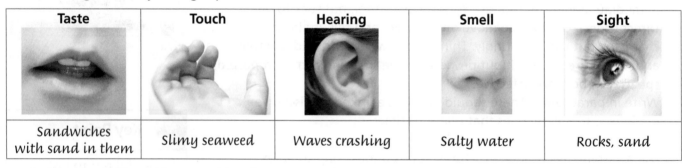				
Sandwiches with sand in them	Slimy seaweed	Waves crashing	Salty water	Rocks, sand

- Another useful way of approaching description is 'big to small', starting with what something is like from a distance and moving in like a camera:

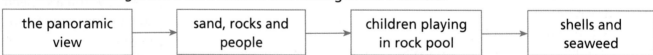

| the panoramic view | → | sand, rocks and people | → | children playing in rock pool | → | shells and seaweed |

Language and Style

- Consider whether to use the first or third person – you may or may not want to describe personal feelings:

  – *I feel a huge sense of regret as the train leaves.*

- Decide whether to write in the present or past tense: they can be equally effective but you should stick to one.
- Use **imagery** and figurative language, including metaphors and similes:

  – *The train roared like an angry lion.*

Key Point

When you describe something, remember that you can use all five senses.

- Use adjectives and adverbs:

  - *The deep mysterious sea*
  - *The engine spluttered fitfully.*

- Be adventurous in your choice of vocabulary. Use words that have precise, rather than general, meanings. Does the man walk across the road? Or does he amble, trot, stride or even swagger?
- Use techniques such as alliteration, assonance and onomatopoeia:

  - *sparkling, shining sea*
  - *gloomy blue rooms*
  - *the fizz and pop of the fireworks*

- Use both active and passive voices:

  - *A dark forest surrounded the cottage.*
  - *The cottage is surrounded by a dark forest.*

- Write in paragraphs. Vary their length and link them with a variety of discourse markers:

  - *Beyond this lies a flat, wide bog.*
  - *But these sights were as nothing to what lay beyond.*

- Vary your sentence lengths and use techniques such as **parallel phrasing**. This is the use of phrases constructed in the same way and arranged in pairs or sequences:

  - *Tiny rivulets run down the lane; a massive lake covers the fields.*

Example
- This description of a person uses some of the techniques described above.

> George lived alone. Gnarled and weather-beaten, he looked older than his sixty years: his skin was sun-baked and blemished; his forehead grooved with deep furrows; his few remaining teeth black and crooked, like ancient gravestones. His teeth were rarely seen, for he had few reasons to smile. His one companion was his terrier Barney, whom he loved. In return Barney offered unquestioning love, loyalty and apparent affection.

> **Key Point**
>
> If the task is to write a description, do not write a story.

It is written in the past tense and the third person.

It describes George's appearance but also gives us some background.

The imagery is mainly literal but figurative imagery is also used.

Both active and passive voices are used.

There is a variety of sentence structures.

> **Quick Test**
>
> Look at the example above. Find examples of:
> 1. A simple sentence.
> 2. A simile.
> 3. Alliteration.
> 4. The passive voice.

> **Key Words**
>
> imagery
> parallel phrasing

Reading Non-fiction 1

You must be able to:

- Read and understand a range of non-fiction texts
- Compare writers' ideas and perspectives.

Form, Purpose and Audience

- Your texts could come from a number of **non-fiction forms** and **genres**. The most likely are discussed below.
- Think about the writer's purpose. It could be to describe, to inform and explain, to argue, to persuade or to advise. Remember that a text can have more than one purpose.
- Think about the intended audience. It might be aimed at people of a certain age: for example, children, teenagers, older people. It could be intended for people in a particular job or with particular interests: for example, doctors, gardeners, cyclists. It might, however, be written for a general audience or with no audience in mind.

Key Point

Non-fiction is any writing that is not made up by the writer. It is not necessarily fact but it is what the writer believes to be true.

Diaries

- Diaries and **journals** are very personal. They are written by people who want to keep a record of what they have done and to express their opinions and feelings about what is happening around them.
- They can seem very immediate and spontaneous. We expect to get a genuine, uncensored and sincere point of view. They also give us an insight into what people really did and thought in the past.
- However, many diaries have been edited. We can still learn what the writer thought at the time of writing but it may not be exactly what he or she wrote. Some diaries may have been written with publication in mind by writers conscious of giving their 'version' of events.
- Diaries can vary a lot in style. Some use chatty, **informal language**. Others are quite formal. Some **diarists** jot down impressions and thoughts in a quite disorganized way. Other diaries are considered and crafted.

Letters

- Letters can give us an insight into people's everyday lives. Their style and tone depend a lot on their purpose.
- Letters give news and opinions, discuss ideas and express feelings. Letters might also be asking for something (like a job), complaining about something, or thanking someone for something.
- Unlike diarists, letter writers are always conscious of their audience. A letter to a close friend would be different in tone, style and content

from a letter to a grandmother. It would be very different from a letter to a newspaper about current events, or to a prospective employer.

- The tone of a letter – friendly, angry, ironic, cold – will tell you a lot about the relationship between the writer and the **recipient** at the time of writing.

Autobiography and Biography

- **Biography** means writing about life. **Autobiography** means writing about one's own life.
- An autobiography can be reflective, even 'confessional', as the writer considers his or her past actions. It may also be self-justifying, naive or downright untrue. Autobiographies written by current celebrities (or their 'ghostwriters') are often written with the purpose of promoting the subject's career.
- Biographies range from what are known as 'hatchet jobs', designed to ruin their subjects' reputations, to 'hagiographies' (originally written about saints), which have nothing but good to say. Most are something in between.
- A biographer's point of view may come from his or her own relationship with the subject. On the other hand, it might be based on a careful consideration of the evidence.

Key Point

Many non-fiction texts use 'literary' techniques associated with fiction. Some exam boards (WJEC Eduqas and OCR) include 'literary non-fiction', such as biographical and autobiographical writing, in the same exam as fiction texts. AQA and Edexcel have one exam on fiction and one on non-fiction texts.

Key Words

non-fiction
form
genre
journal
informal language
diarist
recipient
biography
autobiography

Quick Test

Where are you most likely to find the following?
1. An account of someone's whole life.
2. Thanks for a present.
3. The writer's secret feelings.
4. How the writer became a megastar.

Reading Non-fiction 2

You must be able to:

- Read and understand a range of non-fiction texts
- Compare writers' ideas and perspectives.

Travel Writing

- Travel writing includes newspaper and magazine **articles** about places to visit, which give readers opinions and advice about a place. These are similar to reviews.
- You are more likely to be given **autobiographical** accounts of more adventurous trips – a journey down the Amazon or climbing a mountain in the Himalayas. These contain information about the places described but are more concerned with the personal experience of challenge and adventure.
- Some writers might seem awestruck and/or delighted by everything they encounter. Others are more critical, especially when writing about people and their way of life. They might even give opinions on political or other controversial issues.
- Some writers use the techniques of fiction writers to build suspense and involve readers. Others go in for colourful, even poetic description. Some write wittily about their reactions to new experiences.
- Some writers are experts, perhaps using a lot of unfamiliar terminology, for example, about mountaineering. Others see themselves as naive travellers – 'innocents abroad' – who tell jokes at their own expense.

Key Point

Sources in your exam could include blogs, internet reviews or other texts taken from the internet. You should approach these in the same way as any other text.

Journalism

- **Journalism** is anything that is published in a newspaper or magazine.
- Newspaper **reports** give the news and are mainly factual. **Features** – in both newspapers and magazines – look at issues in more depth. Sometimes they are balanced discussions. They can, however, strongly argue for a point of view.
- Articles can be serious or amusing. Most newspapers have regular feature writers. Some of them write about themselves and their families in a way that encourages readers to empathize with them. Others focus on more controversial issues.
- Most magazines are aimed at particular readerships – for example, women, men, teenagers, older people.
- Newspapers are aimed at a general, adult audience. However, different newspapers have different readerships, often associated with particular political views.

Reviews

- A **review** is an article that gives a point of view about, for example, a film, book, concert, game or restaurant.

- Reviews give information, such as venue, date, time and price. Their main purpose, however, is to give the writer's point of view.
- Some reviews are quite balanced, giving positive and negative views, though they usually do arrive at a judgement. Others express their views very strongly, sometimes in a witty way.

Comparing Views and Attitudes

- In your exam you will be asked to compare two **sources**. These will be about similar subjects but written from different points of view.
- You should discuss what similarities and/or differences there are between the writers' attitudes:

> *Smith feels that we need to save rural areas, whereas Jones is happy for towns to expand.*

- The attitudes shown in the sources might be directly stated or implied:

> *While Williams is shocked at the idea of women doing 'men's work', Roberts seems not to share the view as she does not comment on the fact that the engineer is a woman.*

- Think about the impression you get of the writer:

> *Jones is clearly an expert on the subject, while Smith writes as a confused voter.*

- Consider the general tone:

> *Williams uses humour to make his point, but Roberts writes seriously about her emotions.*

- Remember to comment on structure and language:

> *Jones's use of subheadings breaks the article into clear 'points', making it more accessible.*

> *Smith uses slang, trying to appeal to young readers, whereas Jones uses formal, quite technical language.*

- And remember that you are being asked to compare the writers' views, not to give your own.

Quick Test

In which of the following are you least likely to find the writer's point of view?
1. A review.
2. A news report.
3. A feature.
4. Travel writing.

Writing Non-fiction 1

You must be able to:

- Communicate clearly, effectively and imaginatively
- Adapt your writing for different forms, purposes and audiences.

The Task

- In your exam you will be given the opportunity to express your views on a theme explored in the reading section of the exam.
- You will be given a statement or scenario, and instructions which include details of purpose, form and **audience**:

> 'School holidays create problems for parents and damage children's education.'
>
> Write an article for a student website in which you argue for or against this view.

Audience

- Sometimes the task specifies an audience:
  - Write a letter to your head teacher.
- Sometimes the audience is implied by the form:
  - Write a speech for your school assembly.
- Your intended audience determines what sort of language you use. Think about whether a formal or informal tone is called for.
- You would write informally for people you know well, using the sort of language that you use when chatting with them. However, you should avoid using 'text language' (**abbreviations**, emoticons etc.) in the exam.
- It can be appropriate to write informally for people you don't know, as if you were their friend, for example, in a magazine article aimed at teenagers.
- For almost everything else use a formal tone and write in Standard English (see pages 14–15).
- Whether you are writing formally or informally, be aware of your audience's interests and points of view. For example, if you were writing for a local audience you would focus on known local concerns:

> *Here in Bingley, we have always been proud of our green spaces.*

- You would expect school governors to be concerned about the school's reputation:

> *I know that you are just as concerned as I am about recent complaints of unsocial behaviour.*

- And a little flattery can go a long way:

> *I have always been impressed by your commitment to our community.*

Key Point

If you are doing the WJEC Eduqas exams, you will be required to complete two pieces of writing. For all other exam boards, you should do only one writing task.

- You are free to agree or disagree with the stimulus you are given. The important thing is to try to convince the reader of your view.

Purpose

- The purpose of your writing is usually to express your point of view. The wording of the task might give a slightly different emphasis. For example, 'argue' sounds more passionate than 'explain', while 'persuade' suggests more emphasis on the audience. 'Advise' implies that you know more about the subject than your audience and that you should suggest practical solutions to problems.

Constructing an Argument

- In constructing your **argument**, start with a powerful opening paragraph, which grabs your audience and makes your point clear.
- Make sure you offer a number of points in support of your argument, starting a new paragraph for each.
- Acknowledge other points of view but then give your **counter-arguments**, pointing out why you think they are wrong:

> *Some people argue that school uniforms stifle individuality. However,...*

- Structure your argument in a logical order, using **discourse markers** to 'signpost' the development of your argument:

> *Another point I would like to make is...*

- Back up your points with evidence if you can. You can use the sources for the reading question to help you with this.
- Give appropriate examples, including **anecdotes**:

> *Only last week, I encountered such behaviour...*

- Address your audience directly (**direct address**), using 'you', and show your own involvement by using 'I' and 'we'.
- Use a full range of **rhetorical devices**, including lists of three, repetition and **hyperbole** (see pages 28–29).
- Use humour if you think it is appropriate.
- Use a variety of sentence structures, and use the passive as well as the active voice.
- Finish with a strong conclusion, summing up the main points and strongly stating your opinion.

> **Quick Test**

Look at this task:
Your head teacher has banned packed lunches. Write to the governors giving your reaction. What is its:
1. purpose
2. audience
3. form?

Writing Non-fiction 2

You must be able to:

- Communicate clearly, effectively and imaginatively
- Adapt your writing for different forms, purposes and audiences.

Form: Articles

- You could be asked to write an article for a newspaper, magazine or website.
- If it is a newspaper, the task might specify whether it is a broadsheet, tabloid or local newspaper.
- Broadsheets are 'serious' newspapers, which look at news in more detail and depth, such as the *Daily Telegraph* and *The Guardian.*
- Tabloids, like *The Sun* and the *Daily Mirror*, cover news in less depth and devote more space to things like celebrity gossip.
- Tabloids use short paragraphs and sentences, and simple vocabulary. Broadsheets use longer paragraphs and sentences, and more sophisticated vocabulary.

- Do not try to make your answer look like a newspaper or magazine. There are no marks for design. Do not include:
  - a masthead (the newspaper's title)
  - columns
  - illustrations
  - any articles apart from the one you have been asked to write.
- You can, however, include organizational devices such as:
  - a headline – perhaps using alliteration ('Ban this Beastly Business'), a pun or a play on words ('A Tale of Two Kitties'). But don't put it in huge coloured letters!
  - a strapline, under the headline, expanding on or explaining the headline ('Why We Should Boycott Cosmetics')
  - subheadings – to guide the reader through the text.
- You must write in paragraphs.
- Magazine and website articles are similar to newspaper articles in form.

Key Point

You are not likely to be asked to write a tabloid article: it would not give you enough scope to demonstrate your skills.

Form: Letters

- There are a number of 'rules' or conventions that are used in letter-writing. These are often not used in informal letters.
- If you are asked to write a letter in the exam, it will probably be quite formal.

Example of How to Open a Letter

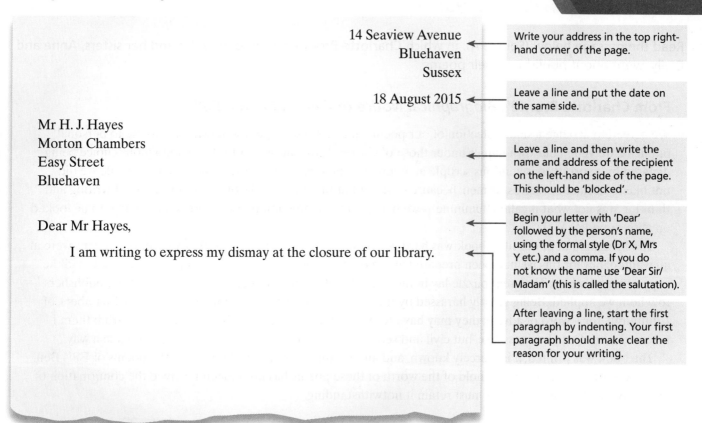

14 Seaview Avenue
Bluehaven
Sussex

18 August 2015

Mr H. J. Hayes
Morton Chambers
Easy Street
Bluehaven

Dear Mr Hayes,

    I am writing to express my dismay at the closure of our library.

Write your address in the top right-hand corner of the page.

Leave a line and put the date on the same side.

Leave a line and then write the name and address of the recipient on the left-hand side of the page. This should be 'blocked'.

Begin your letter with 'Dear' followed by the person's name, using the formal style (Dr X, Mrs Y etc.) and a comma. If you do not know the name use 'Dear Sir/Madam' (this is called the salutation).

After leaving a line, start the first paragraph by indenting. Your first paragraph should make clear the reason for your writing.

- Continue with paragraphs that make further relevant points before ending with one that tells the reader what you would like to happen next.
- Connect your paragraphs with discourse markers.
- If you have addressed the reader by name, sign off with 'Yours sincerely'. If you haven't, use 'Yours faithfully'.
- Remember the 'five Cs':
  - Clear – Say what you mean in good English.
  - Complete – Include everything necessary, giving enough detail and explaining your points properly.
  - Concise – Don't 'ramble'. Do not include irrelevant information or ideas.
  - Correct – Say what you believe to be true.
  - Courteous – Be polite. Consider the recipient and his or her possible reaction to your letter.

 Key Point

Unless you are writing informally for young people, avoid slang or dialect words, contractions and abbreviations.

 Quick Test

How should you end a letter beginning with the following salutations?
1. Dear Mr Blenkinsop
2. Dear Principal
3. Dear Madam
4. Dear Sir Arthur

 Key Words

broadsheet
tabloid
headline
pun
strapline
subheading

Read the passage below (Source A), in which Charlotte Brontë describes how she and her sisters, Anne and Emily, went about publishing their poems.

From Charlotte Brontë's *Biographical Notice of Ellis and Acton Bell*

We agreed to arrange a small selection of our poems, and, if possible, get them printed. Averse to personal publicity, we veiled our own names under those of Currer, Ellis, and Acton Bell; the ambiguous choice being dictated by a sort of conscientious scruple at assuming Christian names positively masculine, while we did not like to declare ourselves women, because – without at that time suspecting that our mode of writing and thinking was not what is called 'feminine' – we had a vague impression that authoresses are liable to be looked on with prejudice [...]

The bringing out of our little book was hard work. As was to be expected, neither we nor our poems were at all wanted; but for this we had been prepared at the outset; though inexperienced ourselves, we had read the experience of others. The great puzzle lay in the difficulty of getting answers of any kind from the publishers to whom we applied. Being greatly harassed by this obstacle I ventured to apply to the Messrs. Chambers, of Edinburgh, for a word of advice; they may have forgotten the circumstance, but I have not, for from them I received a brief and business-like, but civil and sensible reply, on which we acted, and at last made a way.

The book was printed; it is scarcely known, and all of it that merits to be known are the poems of Ellis Bell. The fixed conviction I held, and hold of the worth of these poems has not indeed received the confirmation of much favourable criticism; but I must retain it notwithstanding.

1 What was Charlotte Brontë's pseudonym?

_____ [1]

2 Brontë says they were 'averse' to publicity. Select one definition from the list below that best defines 'averse'.

a) enthusiastic

b) opposed

c) attracted

d) indifferent

_____ [1]

3 What does Brontë mean by saying that their choice of names was ambiguous?

_____ [1]

4 Why did they choose these names?

_____ [1]

5 Why has she not forgotten the reply from Messrs Chambers?

_____ [1]

6 Now read this article (Source B). Compare Brontë's and Fordyce's experiences of trying to become writers.

How I Made My Own Luck

by Lily Fordyce

People often ask me for advice about writing, which really means they want me to give them the magic key that opens the door to publication, fame and fortune. I can't promise any of that. All I can do is say how it was for me, and that what worked for me won't work for everyone. There are two essential ingredients: hard work and luck. Some people say you make your own luck. If that's true, this is the luck I made:

1. I started reading out my poetry in public. It wasn't that hard for me. I'm one of life's show-offs. I was welcomed with enthusiasm, especially because I'm a woman. 'We don't get enough women' was a cry I heard again and again.

2. I sent my poems to every poetry magazine going, whether they pay or not (mostly they don't) and very soon I was seeing my work in print.

3. I entered almost every competition I could find.

And finally, I won a competition, which led to my first book, which did very well – and here I am: a hardworking and very lucky poet.

_____

_____

_____

_____

_____

_____

_____

_____

_____ [8]

7 Look again at Source B. Explore how Fordyce uses language to convey her feelings about becoming a poet.

Refer to the text. Write your answer on a separate piece of paper. [12]

Reading

Source A

Source A is an article from *The Times* newspaper, 15 May 1914.

The Cult of Little Dogs: An Irresistible Appeal by Our Correspondent

There is a certain melancholy attaching to shows of toy dogs. Not that toy dogs are themselves melancholy – indeed it is their sprightly unconsciousness of their degeneracy that most confounds the moralist – but that they suggest melancholy reflections. The Englishman, perhaps alone among the peoples of the world, understands fully the great soul of the dog; he feels his own kinship with it – as he did in former days with that of the fighting cock; and he has accepted with pride the bull-dog as the type of his national qualities. It is not, then, without misgiving that he watches the process of minimizing the dog, or a large proportion of him, in an eager competition to crib, cabin, and confine the great soul in the smallest possible body, until, in place of the dignified friend and ally of man, there will be left nothing but, at worst, a pampered toy; at best, a pathetic creature, all eyes and nerves, whose insurgent soul frets the puny body to decay.

Where will the process end? Already we have held up to the admiration of the world a Pomeranian puppy which, at the age of three months, can be comfortably bestowed in a tumbler, over the edge of which his picture shows him looking, with shy eyes and apprehensively, at the disproportionate scheme of things. Presently, maybe, we shall have a childhood's dream realized and really see the little dog of the fairy-story who was hidden in a walnut and, when the shell was cracked, leapt forth barking and wagging his tail to the delight of all the noble company.

Source B

Source B is a letter to a newspaper.

14 Raglan Terrace
Tillingbourne

12 July 2015

Dear Editor,

I was saddened to read yet more negative coverage of so-called 'purse pets' in your paper. What is it about celebrities who own small dogs that inspires such vitriol?

I know some people think celebrities use their pets as fashion accessories – and this is questionable. But it is not, as you suggest, cruel. We like to think of our four-legged friends as free and independent spirits – equal companions on life's journey – but they're not. Dogs depend on us for food, shelter and love.

This is the case whether they are tiny little chihuahuas that can fit in a Versace handbag or massive Afghans – or even breeds like pit bulls. Now, I don't want to be accused of the kind of prejudice I'm criticizing others for, but let's just reflect for a moment. Which is crueller? Pampering your pet with little treats or training her to fight and kill other dogs?

Of course, I'm not saying that all Staffie owners do this. But you should not imply that everyone who owns a little dog is cruel. Taking dogs shopping for little doggy clothes is a bit silly, but it does not damage their health or well-being. On the contrary, it shows that the owners care about their pets. In fact, many celebrity dog owners go further to show they care. Actress Kristin Chenoweth has even founded a charity, named after her tiny Maltese, to help homeless pets.

These dogs are beautiful, loyal and lovable. I know. I've got one. I don't keep her in my handbag or take her to canine boutiques, but I love and cherish her – and I wouldn't be without her. I don't think you'd write an article castigating me for those feelings, so why aim your vitriol at Paris Hilton and Mariah Carey, whose only crime is to love their pets?

Yours faithfully

Joanna P. Hanlon

1 Refer only to Source A.

How does the writer use language and structure to express his feelings about small dogs?

_____

_____

_____

_____

_____

_____

_____

_____ [12]

2 Refer to both Source A and Source B.

'In these texts the writers display very different attitudes to small dogs.'

How far do you agree with this statement?

In your answer you should:
* discuss your impression of the writers' feelings
* compare the ways in which the writers present their feelings
* support your ideas with quotations from both texts.

Write your answer on a separate piece of paper. [18]

Writing

3 'A dog is for life, not just for Christmas.'

Write an article for a magazine aimed at people your own age, inspired by this quotation, in which you give your views about dogs, dog owners, or both.

Write on a separate piece of paper.

[24 marks for content and organization, 16 marks for technical accuracy; total 40]

Context

You must be able to:

- Understand the social, historical and cultural context of a Shakespeare play
- Use this understanding to evaluate the play.

History

- The historical **context** in which Shakespeare lived was very different from ours.
- He lived from 1564 to 1616 and started writing during the reign of Queen Elizabeth I, a time of great prosperity for England, when explorers were discovering and colonizing new lands across the world. Such adventures inspired *The Tempest*.
- There was also a great flowering of literature and theatre, inspired by the Renaissance in Italy.
- In 1603 Elizabeth I was succeeded by King James I, who was already King of Scotland. He became patron of Shakespeare's theatre company and *Macbeth* was written in his honour.

Religion

- England was an overwhelmingly Christian country. The official church was the Church of England, but many people were still Roman Catholics, while others (like Puritans) had stricter Protestant beliefs.
- Most people believed that after death God would judge them and decide whether they should spend eternity in Heaven or Hell. The idea of Hell is ever-present in *Macbeth.*
- The general attitude to non-Christians is reflected in the way other characters treat Shylock in *The Merchant of Venice*, although some would say that Shakespeare's writing causes the audience to question their assumptions.
- Many people also believed in astrology. The tension between the popular belief that everything is mapped out in the stars and the Christian belief in free will is present in many plays. We see this in *Romeo and Juliet*. Astrology is also prominent in *Julius Caesar*.

> **Key Point**
>
> Elizabethans and Jacobeans would have recognized the many biblical references found in Shakespeare.

Morality

- Society's moral and ethical standards were rooted in Christian teaching and the Ten Commandments.
- Most people shared similar ideas about sexual **morality**. Chastity, especially among women, was much more highly prized than in today's society and marriage was for life. This idea is central to *Much Ado About Nothing, Othello* and *Romeo and Juliet.*

Social Order

- Many people believed that the **social order**, with the King or Queen at the top, was derived from God and should not be tampered with.
- King James believed in 'the **divine right** of kings'.
  - This is a major theme in *Macbeth.*
  - The rights and wrongs of opposing rulers are also a theme of *Julius Caesar* and *The Tempest.*
- The **authority** of parents over children might also be seen as sacred, although this authority is challenged in *Romeo and Juliet* and *Othello.*

Society

- Although there was a parliament, England was not democratic in the modern sense.
- Political power centred on the **court**, around the Queen or King. Here, aristocrats competed for the monarch's favour.
- There was a growing middle class. Shakespeare was the son of a well-off glover from Stratford-upon-Avon. He benefited from a good education at the local grammar school. In these schools boys studied ancient history and Latin literature, the source of *Julius Caesar.*
- Most people, however, were illiterate. Many worked on the land, although cities were expanding. London's thriving port attracted merchants and travellers from all over the world.
- Women were usually dependent on their husbands or fathers, so making the right marriage was important. However, there were examples of rich and powerful women.
  - Olivia in *Twelfth Night* and Portia in *The Merchant of Venice* have both inherited their wealth. While both are clearly in command of their households, Portia still cannot choose her own husband.
- Many of Shakespeare's female characters, like Beatrice in *Much Ado About Nothing*, show themselves to be equal to men. However, Portia and Viola (in *Twelfth Night*), in disguising themselves as men, and Lady Macbeth, in her desire to be 'unsexed', are conscious of taking on a 'man's role'.

Key Point

It is important to understand the differences between Shakespeare's society and ours.

Quick Test

True or False?
1. *Macbeth* was written for Queen Elizabeth.
2. Astrology is a Christian belief.
3. Divorce was common in Shakespeare's time.
4. James I believed that his authority came from God.

Key Words

context
morality
social order
divine right
authority
court

Themes

You must be able to:

- Identify themes in a Shakespeare play
- Write about how Shakespeare presents themes.

Themes and Ideas

- A theme is part of the subject matter of a text – a concern that runs through the play.
- Shakespeare's plays are full of ideas about relationships, morality and society.
- Your exam question could focus on themes and ideas:
  - Explain how Shakespeare presents the idea of kingship in *Henry V*.
  - Write about how Shakespeare explores ideas about love in *Romeo and Juliet*.

Identifying Themes

- Throughout his career, Shakespeare would return to the same themes. Here are some themes that occur frequently in his plays:

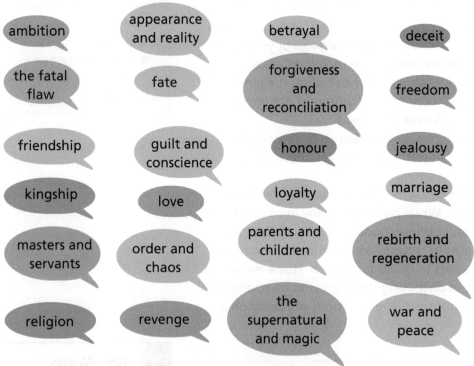

ambition · appearance and reality · betrayal · deceit · the fatal flaw · fate · forgiveness and reconciliation · freedom · friendship · guilt and conscience · honour · jealousy · kingship · love · loyalty · marriage · masters and servants · order and chaos · parents and children · rebirth and regeneration · religion · revenge · the supernatural and magic · war and peace

> **Key Point**
>
> Shakespeare uses his characters and plots to explore issues that mattered to people at the time he wrote. Most of them still matter.

- You may think of more. In over 30 plays Shakespeare looked at almost every aspect of human life.
- Write down some themes that occur in the play you have studied. Try to find at least five. Here are some to get you started:
  - *Macbeth* – marriage…
  - *Much Ado About Nothing* – misunderstandings…
  - *The Merchant of Venice* – the outsider…
  - *The Tempest* – freedom…

- *Romeo and Juliet* – betrayal…
- *Henry V* – war…
- *Othello* – jealousy…
- *Twelfth Night* – disguise…

- Now write a sentence or two about each theme:

> Ambition is an important theme in 'Julius Caesar' because Caesar is killed when he achieves his ambition to rule Rome alone. The conspirators are also ambitious and their ambitions also destroy them.
>
> Forgiveness and reconciliation are central to 'The Tempest'. Prospero has his enemies at his mercy but chooses not to have his revenge on them.

How Themes are Presented

- Shakespeare's plays have been interpreted in many different ways over the past 400 years. You must come to your own conclusions about his themes by considering the evidence.
- Think about the **plot** – what happens in the play:
  - Macbeth's murder of Duncan brings together the themes of ambition and kingship.
  - The theme of friendship comes to the fore in *Much Ado About Nothing* when Beatrice asks Benedick to kill his friend Claudio because of how he has treated Hero.
- Theatre is a visual medium. Shakespeare presents us with powerful **images**:
  - The appearance of Banquo's ghost in *Macbeth* speaks volumes about betrayal and guilt.
  - Juliet's appearance on a balcony above Romeo demonstrates the kind of love that he has for her.
- **Dialogue** can give us insight into themes by presenting more than one point of view:
  - The trial scene in *The Merchant of Venice* gives us both Shylock's and Antonio's views about business ethics.
  - In *Julius Caesar* idealist Brutus and pragmatist Cassius debate the rights and wrongs of their actions. We might side with one or the other, or feel that there is a middle way.
- Characters can raise themes and **issues** when they speak directly to the audience in a soliloquy or aside. When they do this they reveal what they really think:
  - Macbeth shares his doubts about killing Duncan. His soliloquies draw us into a consideration of the themes of kingship, loyalty and ambition.
  - In *The Tempest* Prospero tells us he intends to give up his 'rough magic', making us think about power and old age.

 Key Point

Shakespeare does not tell us what he thinks or what we should think. There are more questions than answers.

 Quick Test

Give a single word defined by the following:
1. A speech made to the audience.
2. Speech between two or more people.
3. What happens in the play.
4. A concern that runs through the play.

 Key Words

theme
plot
image
dialogue
issue

Characters

You must be able to:

- Write about how Shakespeare presents characters.

Characters

- Shakespeare is known for his huge range of characters and his understanding of human psychology.
- Your exam question might focus on characters' relationships with each other:
  - In what ways is Emilia an important character in *Othello*?
  - Write about how far you think Shakespeare presents Shylock as a victim.
  - Explore how Shakespeare presents Viola's relationship with Sebastian in *Twelfth Night*.
- You may be asked to analyse how Shakespeare presents the character or relationship in a short extract from the play, in the play as a whole, or both.
- When revising, think about each character's:
  - background
  - personality
  - relationships
  - **motivation**
  - function in the plot.
- Identify the main characters in your play and draw up a chart like the (partially completed) one below:

> **Key Point**
>
> When looking at characters, consider their historical and social context.

Character	Background	Personality	Relationships	Motivation	Function
Romeo	The son of the Capulets			Wants to be with Juliet whatever the cost	
Juliet		Innocent but very determined			
Capulet			Loves his family but expects obedience		
Nurse		Chatty, bawdy, devoted, pragmatic			Juliet's confidante – but advises her to forget Romeo

- The main characters all find themselves in different situations by the end of the play. How did they get there and how did their experiences change them?
- Try tracing your characters' development through events that have influenced them. Here is an example for Macbeth.

What happens?	What effect does it have?
He meets the witches.	He starts to think about his future and possibly becoming king.

He kills Duncan.	He becomes king. He has power but fears losing it and turns against Banquo.
He sees Banquo's ghost.	He feels guilty and acts strangely.
He visits the witches.	He fears losing his crown, which makes him more ruthless.
Malcolm invades Scotland.	Thinking he is invincible, he becomes defiant and brave.

How Characters are Presented

What They Say

- A **soliloquy** is a speech to the audience, usually with no other characters on stage. Soliloquies let us into characters' thought processes, revealing a lot about their character and motivation:
  - Juliet shows her excitement and impatience when waiting for the Nurse to return from seeing Romeo.
- Sometimes characters comment briefly on what others are saying and doing in an **aside**. We can assume they mean what they say.
- Characters do not always tell the truth. All Shakespeare plays include people who lie to others.
- We do not, however, have to guess who is lying. It is clear when someone cannot be trusted:
  - Lady Macbeth tells Macbeth to 'look like the innocent flower / But be the serpent under't'.

What Others Say

- We learn about characters through what others say to and about them.
- Sometimes we get a consensus of opinion:
  - Macbeth changes from being universally praised for his bravery and loyalty to being hated and feared as a 'devil' and 'fiend'.
- A difference of opinion can give us something to think about:
  - The violent Tybalt in *Romeo and Juliet* is a favourite of both Lady Capulet and the Nurse. This tells us about both his character and theirs.
- Always be aware of who the speaker is:
  - Antony's description of Brutus, in *Julius Caesar*, as 'the noblest Roman of them all' carries more weight because of their enmity.

How They Act and React

- We learn about characters by their actions:
  - When Bassanio chooses the lead casket in *The Merchant of Venice* we know he is genuine.
- Their reactions also reveal a lot:
  - Benedick's reaction to Beatrice's command to 'kill Claudio' reveals his growing feelings for her, and tells us about his sense of honour.

> **Key Point**
>
> When Shakespeare wants us to know what characters are really thinking and feeling, they speak to the audience.

 Quick Test

True or False?
1. Everyone tells the truth.
2. Characters never address the audience.
3. Characters can change.
4. We can get differing views of a character.

> **Key Words**
>
> motivation
> soliloquy
> aside

Language and Structure

You must be able to:

- Analyse Shakespeare's use of language and structure
- Use relevant terminology.

Verse and Prose

- Shakespeare wrote in a mixture of **verse** and **prose**. Most of his verse is in **iambic pentameter**. 'Pentameter' means there are five stressed syllables on every line. 'Iambic' refers to the stress falling on every second syllable:

  > O, **she** doth **teach** the **torch**es **to** shine **bright**.

- It is often said that the iambic pentameter follows the natural rhythms of speech and that it resembles a heartbeat.
- Sometimes Shakespeare varies the **metre** to emphasize certain words: for example, stressing the first syllable in a line or adding an extra syllable. He might create a pause (known as a **caesura**) in the middle of the line.
- **Rhyming couplets** might end a scene or emphasize an important thought.
- Other metres are occasionally used in Shakespeare, for example in songs.
- Verse tends to be used for higher-status characters when discussing serious things. However, much of the banter in *Much Ado About Nothing* is in prose. Characters such as servants usually speak in prose, but there are exceptions, as in Caliban's description of the island.

Structure

- Shakespeare's plays are divided into five acts. The first introduces the characters and their concerns. Then something happens that changes the characters' lives. In the third act things become more complicated. The fourth act tends to be about the complications being sorted out. The final act brings a resolution and the play ends with the restoration of order.
- When focusing on an extract think about which part of the play it comes from and how it fits into the play as a whole.
- Think about how Shakespeare uses contrasting scenes. He sometimes uses comic scenes to release tension before building to a tragic climax: for example, the 'porter scene' in *Macbeth*.

Imagery

- Shakespeare's imagery tells us about characters, creates mood and underlines key themes. His techniques include simile, metaphor and personification.

> **Key Point**
>
> You can tell verse from prose just by looking at it. Verse has definite line endings and a rhythm, often in a regular pattern or metre.

- Sometimes characters use **extended metaphors** or **conceits**. Romeo and Juliet use the **sonnet** form to develop the idea of Romeo being a pilgrim and Juliet a saint.
- Look for patterns of imagery in your play. Animal imagery, much of it connected to the Bible, runs through *The Merchant of Venice*:

> Why he hath made the ewe bleat for the lamb.

Rhetorical Language

- Rhetorical questions are common when characters are wondering what to do:

> I have railed so long against marriage, but doth not the appetite alter?

- Repetition emphasizes important ideas or feelings:

> Tomorrow and tomorrow and tomorrow.

- The 'rule of three' is used by characters trying to convince others:

> Friends, Romans, countrymen, lend me your ears.

- Shakespeare uses rhetorical techniques in situations where they might be used in life, for example in the trial scene in *The Merchant of Venice*.

Playing with Words

- Elizabethans loved experimenting with words. Shakespeare shows this in characters like Romeo, who uses **oxymoron** to express his confusion:

> Feather of lead, bright smoke, cold fire, sick health.

- Romeo also uses puns (double meanings), as do Beatrice and Benedick when they pit their wits against each other.
- Double meanings are often used to make sexual innuendoes.
- Shakespeare also uses techniques such as alliteration and assonance to create feelings and mood:

> Full fathom five thy father lies.

> ### Key Point
>
> Whatever the focus of the question, you must write about Shakespeare's language in your answer.

> ### Key Words
>
> verse
> prose
> iambic pentameter
> metre
> caesura
> rhyming couplet
> extended metaphor
> conceit
> sonnet
> oxymoron

> ### Quick Test
>
> Of what are the following examples?
> 1. What, must I hold a candle to my shames?
> 2. Pure impiety and impious purity.
> 3. O mighty Caesar! Dost thou lie so low?
> 4. Hence will I to my ghostly sire's close cell,
>   His help to crave and my dear hap to tell.

Reading

Read the passage below and then answer the questions.

In this extract from *The Hound of the Baskervilles* by Sir Arthur Conan Doyle, Dr Mortimer is telling Sherlock Holmes and Dr Watson about the death of Sir Charles Baskerville, who believed his family was cursed and haunted by a mysterious beast.

'It was at my advice that Sir Charles was about to go to London. His heart was, I knew, affected, and the constant anxiety in which he lived, however chimerical[1] the cause of it might be, was evidently having a serious effect upon his health. I thought that a few months among the distractions of town would send him back a new man. Mr Stapleton, a mutual friend who was much concerned at his state of health, was of the same opinion. At the last instant came this terrible catastrophe.

'On the night of Sir Charles's death Barrymore, the butler who made the discovery, sent Perkins the groom on horseback to me, and as I was sitting up late I was able to reach Baskerville Hall within an hour of the event. I checked and corroborated all the facts which were mentioned at the inquest. I followed the footsteps down the yew alley, I saw the spot at the moor-gate where he seemed to have waited, I remarked the change in the shape of the prints after that point, I noted that there were no other footsteps save those of Barrymore on the soft gravel, and finally I carefully examined the body, which had not been touched until my arrival. Sir Charles lay on his face, his arms out, his fingers dug into the ground, and his features convulsed with some strong emotion to such an extent that I could hardly have sworn to his identity. There was certainly no physical injury of any kind. But one false statement was made by Barrymore at the inquest. He said that there were no traces upon the ground round the body. He did not observe any. But I did – some little distance off, but fresh and clear.'

'Footprints?'

'Footprints.'

'A man's or a woman's?'

Dr Mortimer looked strangely at us for an instant, and his voice sank almost to a whisper as he answered:

'Mr Holmes, they were the footprints of a gigantic hound!'

---

[1] *chimerical* – fanciful or imagined

1. This extract comes from the end of the second chapter of *The Hound of the Baskervilles*, a detective story featuring Sherlock Holmes.

   How has the writer structured the text to interest you as a reader?

   You could write about:
   - how Dr Mortimer builds up to the discovery of the body
   - how the information about the footprints is revealed
   - any other structural features that interest you.

_____

_____

_____

_____ [8]

2 Look at the whole text.

What impression do you get of the narrator and his story?

- Write about your impressions of Dr Mortimer and his story.
- Evaluate how the writer has created these impressions.
- Support your opinions with quotations from the text.

Write your answer on a separate piece of paper. [20]

Writing

3 You have been asked to write a creative piece for your school magazine or website.

Either

Write a description suggested by this picture.

Or

Write the opening of a story set in a wild, isolated place. Write on a separate piece of paper.

[24 marks for content and organization; 16 marks for technical accuracy; total 40]

Answer the question on the play you have studied. Write your answer on a separate piece of paper.

1 *Romeo and Juliet* – Read the extract specified and answer the question below.

In this extract, Juliet is waiting for the Nurse to return.

> **Act 2 Scene 5** *Read lines 1–17, from*
>
> JULIET   The clock struck one when I did send the nurse;
>
>   In half an hour she promised to return.
>
> *To*
>
>   But old folks, many feign as they were dead –
>
>   Unwieldy, slow, heavy, and pale as lead.

How does Shakespeare present Romeo and Juliet's love in this speech? Refer closely to the extract in your answer.   [20]

2 *Macbeth* – Read the extract specified and answer the question below.

In this extract, Macbeth has just been told by the witches that he will be king.

> **Act 1 Scene 3** *Read lines 126–141, from*
>
> MACBETH   Two truths are told
>
>   As happy prologues to the swelling act
>
>   Of the imperial theme.
>
> *To*
>
>   and nothing is
>
>   But what is not.

How does Shakespeare present Macbeth's feelings about power and ambition in this speech? Refer closely to the extract in your answer.   [20]

3 *The Tempest* – Read the extract specified and answer the question below.

In this extract, Ariel has just reported to Prospero that he has carried out his orders and caused the shipwreck.

> **Act 1 Scene 2** *Read lines 243–260, from*
>
> ARIEL   Is there more toil? Since thou dost give me pains,
>
>   Let me remember thee what thou hast promised
>
>   Which is not yet performed me.
>
> *To*
>
> PROSPERO   Thou liest, malignant thing. Hast thou forgot
>
>   The foul witch Sycorax, who with age and envy
>
>   Was grown into a hoop? Hast thou forgot her?

Look at how Prospero and Ariel speak and act in this extract. Write about how Shakespeare presents their relationship. Refer closely to the extract in your answer. [20]

4 **Twelfth Night** – Read the extract specified and answer the question below.
In this extract, at Olivia's house, her servant, Maria, talks to her uncle, Sir Toby Belch, about his behaviour.

> **Act 1 Scene 3** *Read lines 1–41, from*
> SIR TOBY   What a plague means my niece to take the death of her brother thus?
> *To*
> SIR TOBY   […] here comes Sir Andrew Agueface.

Explore how Shakespeare presents Sir Toby and Maria's relationship in this extract. Refer closely to the extract in your answer. [20]

5 **Henry V** – Read the extract specified and answer the question below.
In this extract, the Dauphin has sent Henry a gift of tennis balls.

> **Act 1 Scene 2** *Read lines 259–297, from*
> KING   We are glad the Dauphin is so pleasant with us.
> *To*
>   Convey them with safe conduct. Fare you well.

Look at how Henry speaks and behaves here. What do we learn about Henry as a leader? Refer closely to the extract in your answer. [20]

6 **The Merchant of Venice**
Explore how Shakespeare presents Shylock's relationship with Jessica. Refer to the whole of the play. [20]

7 **Julius Caesar**
Explore how Shakespeare presents the attitudes of Brutus and Cassius to Caesar. Refer to the whole of the play. [20]

8 **Much Ado About Nothing**
To what extent does Shakespeare present Beatrice as an independent woman? Refer to the whole of the play. [20]

9 **Othello**
Write about how Shakespeare presents the relationship between Othello and Desdemona at different points in the play. Refer to the whole of the play. [20]

Context

You must be able to:

- Understand the social, historical and cultural context of a nineteenth-century novel
- Use this understanding to evaluate the text.

Religion and Morality

- In the nineteenth century, Britain was a Christian country, with many more churchgoers than now; religion was part of the fabric of most people's lives. Ministers of religion feature in *Jane Eyre* and *Pride and Prejudice*. Different versions of Christianity are practised in Lantern Yard and Raveloe in *Silas Marner.*
- People tended to share similar ideas about what was acceptable, particularly sexually. Deviations from the norm, like Lydia eloping with Wickham in *Pride and Prejudice*, are shocking.
- Many novels are concerned with right and wrong. Dr Jekyll wants to separate his 'evil' and 'good' sides. In *A Christmas Carol*, Dickens asks his readers to think about what Christmas and Christianity really mean.

Society

- Britain was a very wealthy country with a worldwide empire. Some people made huge fortunes, giving them as much power as the old aristocrats.
- There was a growing middle class of people who had comfortable homes and money to spend – including on novels.
- However, there was also great poverty, especially in towns and cities. With no welfare state and low wages, many people lived in terrible conditions. Dickens and Eliot both wrote about the lives of the poor.
- Social reformers fought against inequality. Dickens's work made people think about social issues.

Gender

- Women did not have a vote (although neither did most men) and their career options were limited. *Pride and Prejudice* is based on the need of middle-class women to find husbands. Jane Eyre has to earn her living as a governess.
- Many writers and thinkers supported women's rights. Mary Shelley's mother, Mary Wollstonecraft, was an early feminist.

Race

- It is unusual to find characters who are not white. Some modern readers are shocked by the attitudes shown to ethnic minorities. They are often seen as wild or savage, like Tonga in *The Sign of Four*, or as exotic and mysterious.

 Key Point

The nineteenth century was a time of great change in Britain. Literature reflected this.

Science

- There were many scientific discoveries and advances. Shelley in *Frankenstein*, Stevenson in *The Strange Case of Dr Jekyll and Mr Hyde* and Wells in *The War of the Worlds* use science as a starting point to consider 'what if', as science fiction writers do today.
- Sherlock Holmes uses a range of methods to solve his cases. Some of his **deductions** might seem fanciful but Conan Doyle was knowledgeable about forensics and Holmes is ahead of his time in using this new science.
- Many writers took an interest in new ideas about **psychology**. Shelley's work reflects current discussion of 'nature and nurture'. Stevenson explores ideas about behaviour and responsibility.

Literature: Movements and Genre

- Novelists were influenced by the Romantic movement, led by poets like Wordsworth. This movement rejected the eighteenth-century taste for order and rationality in favour of an emphasis on personal feelings and nature.
- While Jane Austen belongs more to the eighteenth-century tradition, her characters do reflect the fashion for **sentiment** and poetry.
- Mary Shelley was the wife of the Romantic poet Percy Bysshe Shelley, and her work can be described as Romantic. However, *Frankenstein* is more often described as Gothic, a genre related to Romanticism but more sensational, thrilling its readers with horror and the **supernatural**.
- Brontë, Dickens and Stevenson use elements of the Gothic. *A Christmas Carol* and *The Strange Case of Dr Jekyll and Mr Hyde* both cashed in on the popular taste for ghost stories.
- *The Strange Case of Dr Jekyll and Mr Hyde* also owes something to the increasingly popular detective story, of which Sir Arthur Conan Doyle was the best-known exponent.
- H. G. Wells, author of *The War of the Worlds*, was one of the first science fiction writers.

> **Key Point**
>
> Whatever aspect of a text you are looking at, consider its context.

Quick Test

True or False?
1. All men had the vote.
2. Nobody cared about social injustice.
3. Romantic poets thought feelings mattered.
4. Britain changed a lot during the nineteenth century.

> **Key Words**
>
> deduction
> psychology
> sentiment
> supernatural

Themes

You must be able to:

- Identify themes in a nineteenth-century novel
- Write about how themes are presented.

Identifying Themes

- Here are some themes you will find in the set books.
- Look at the themes of the books you have not studied and think about whether they are also present in your novel.
- *Pride and Prejudice*
  - Marriage: marrying well is vital for the women.
  - Class: the class system is rigid and there is a lot of snobbery but Elizabeth breaks through it.
- *Frankenstein*
  - The pursuit of knowledge: Frankenstein's intellectual curiosity has terrible results.
  - Nature and nurture: the monster's potential for good is destroyed because of the way he is treated.
- *A Christmas Carol*
  - The spirit of Christmas: the 'spirit of Christmas' is the true message of Christianity.
  - Ignorance and Want: the monstrous children are a warning of what will happen if society does not tackle poverty and improve education.
- *Jane Eyre*
  - Women's roles: Jane does not accept an inferior role. She is independent, determined and outspoken.
  - Integrity: Jane remains honest and true to herself, and is rewarded by true love.
- *Great Expectations*
  - Money and ambition: Pip's money creates more problems than it solves.
  - Friendship: affection and loyalty are not always valued, but true friendship wins through.
- *The Strange Case of Dr Jekyll and Mr Hyde*
  - Good and evil: Jekyll's attempts to separate the good and evil parts of himself are doomed to failure.
  - Secrets: Victorian London is full of dark secrets.
- *The Sign of Four*
  - Crime: what makes people commit crimes?
  - Truth: detective stories are about finding the truth, thus making the world safer and better.
- *Silas Marner*
  - The outsider and the community: Silas is an outsider in Raveloe.
  - Religious faith: Silas has lost his faith.

- *The War of the Worlds*
  - Science and technology: technology gives power to those who control it.
  - 'The other': do reactions to the Martians represent how we sometimes see other humans?

How Themes are Presented

- Consider events in the novel:
  - In *Great Expectations* Pip suddenly acquires great wealth. The rest of the novel is about how it changes him.
  - The creation of the monster in *Frankenstein* raises questions about science and people trying to 'play God'.
- Narrators might discuss themes:
  - In *A Christmas Carol* Dickens uses his **authorial voice** to give us his views on social problems.
  - The opening lines of *Pride and Prejudice* tell us straightaway that the novel will be about courtship and marriage.
- Characters can embody themes:
  - Eppie in *Silas Marner* represents innocence and hope.
  - The character of Bertha Rochester in *Jane Eyre* brings together themes of madness and duty.
- Characters discuss themes and **issues**:
  - Elizabeth in *Pride and Prejudice* discusses money, class, love and marriage with her sister Jane, and with Darcy, who has a quite different **perspective** on life.
  - Dr Watson disagrees with Sherlock Holmes about women, Watson being shocked at his friend's misogyny.
- It can be helpful to look for **motifs** in a novel. A motif is an image, idea or situation that recurs through a work, suggesting a theme:
  - Characters in *Frankenstein* find comfort and healing in natural beauty.
  - Fire is a recurring motif in *Jane Eyre*, symbolizing passion as well as moving on the story.
- **Settings** can encapsulate themes:
  - Satis House in *Great Expectations* could symbolize the emptiness of wealth and the gloom of lovelessness.
  - The London of *The Strange Case of Dr Jekyll and Mr Hyde* gives us a sense of the dark side of life.

Key Point

A novel's themes emerge in many ways. Think about the themes of your novel. How do you know they are there?

Quick Test

1. Can a novel have more than one theme?
2. What is a motif?
3. Can a narrator discuss themes and ideas?
4. Can a writer give us differing perspectives on a theme?

Key Words

authorial voice
issue
perspective
motif
setting

Characters

You must be able to:

- Write about how characters are presented in a nineteenth-century novel.

Characters

- Your exam question might focus on a character.
- It could be about a character's personality:
  - How does Austen present Elizabeth as a strong-minded woman?
- Or attitudes and feelings:
  - Explore how Stevenson conveys Jekyll's feelings about good and evil.
- Or relationships:
  - Write about how Conan Doyle presents Watson and Holmes's relationship.

Protagonists

- When the protagonist is also the narrator, we are invited to share the character's thoughts and feelings.
- Jane Eyre, Pip in *Great Expectations* and the narrator in *The War of the Worlds* speak to the readers as if they are looking back over their past, sharing feelings and thoughts as well as experiences.
- Pip can be seen as a **naive narrator**, as he does not understand what is going on. Jane Eyre is more perceptive, even though she does not fully understand everything she experiences.
- Both *Jane Eyre* and *Great Expectations* are accounts of growing up. This sort of novel is known by the German word **Bildungsroman**.
- Victor Frankenstein relates most of his own story, but we do get other perspectives. Part of *The Strange Case of Dr Jekyll and Mr Hyde* is narrated by Jekyll, giving us some insight into his mind and a degree of empathy for him.
- Sherlock Holmes is seen through the eyes of Dr Watson. Conan Doyle keeps him distant, to be admired by the readers as he is by Watson.
- Although Silas Marner, Scrooge and Elizabeth in *Pride* and *Prejudice* do not tell their own stories, the writers give us access to their thoughts and feelings. However, the third-person narrative allows authors to stand aside and comment on their characters.

> **Key Point**
>
> Questions on character are most likely to be about the protagonists, but you should not neglect other characters.

Other Characters

- You could be asked to focus on other characters as individuals or as a group.
- Look at these in terms of:
  - their relationship to the protagonist: for example, Elizabeth Bennet's relationship with her sisters

- their **function** in the novel, perhaps as a way of looking at themes: for example, Shelley's use of the monster to present ideas about nature and nurture
- their **significance** in terms of plot: for example, Miss Havisham's influence on Pip's life.

How Characters are Presented

What They Say

- Characters who are also narrators have plenty to say about their ideas and feelings.
- Those who are not main narrators sometimes express themselves in letters.
- Characters reveal themselves in conversation with other characters. Sometimes this is by what they say, as when the monster confronts Frankenstein. Sometimes it is by how they talk. Mr Collins, in *Pride and Prejudice*, reveals his snobbery by constantly referring to Lady Catherine de Burgh.

What the Narrator Says

- Narrators describe characters' personalities as well as their appearance. In *Great Expectations* Pip, as narrator, describes Estella as 'beautiful and self-possessed'. We see her through his eyes.
- In a third-person narrative, however, we can take comments on characters as being trustworthy and neutral, as when Eliot tells us that 'the good-humoured, affectionate-hearted Godfrey Cass was fast becoming a bitter man'.
- A narrator might go further and describe a character's thoughts and feelings. Jane Austen and George Eliot often take us into their characters' heads.

Key Point

Look for what one character says about another and think about what this tells you about both.

How They Act and React

- As in life, character is best seen through actions. In *Pride and Prejudice* Wickham charms everyone, including Elizabeth and the reader, but when he runs away with Lydia, we can all see him for what he is.
- Reactions are just as important. Darcy's reaction to the elopement of Lydia and Wickham makes Elizabeth and the reader see his true character.

Quick Test

1. Without looking at your novel or your notes, write down the names of as many characters as you can in 10 minutes.

Language and Structure

You must be able to:

- Analyse the use of language and structure in a nineteenth-century novel
- Use relevant terminology.

Structure

- *Jane Eyre* tells Jane's story in chronological order. The novel starts at Gateshead, moves to Lowood school, then Thornfield Hall, on to Moor House and back again to Thornfield. These places represent five stages in Jane's development.
- Dickens divides Pip's 'expectations' into three stages: his childhood in Kent, his life in London as a young man, and his 'growing up' from the return of Magwitch to the end.
- In *A Christmas Carol* each chapter (Stave) is devoted to a different spirit. Dickens uses the power of his spirits to introduce 'flashbacks' to Scrooge's past life and 'flash forwards' to show him how things might turn out.
- In *Silas Marner* George Eliot also uses a flashback to tell us about Silas's history, before jumping 15 years to the point at which she started. She then jumps another 16 years between Part One and Part Two.
- *Pride and Prejudice* uses letters as a form of flashback, filling in details about events in London, for example, which have previously been kept from the reader.
- *Frankenstein* starts with a series of letters, which lead us to Frankenstein's narrative, which in turn includes the creature's narrative. At the end we return to Walton's letters to bring the story up to date. This use of multiple narratives is quite common in the Gothic tradition and 'distances' the story, making it seem almost mythical.
- This technique is also used in *The Strange Case of Dr Jekyll and Mr Hyde*. The third-person narrative focuses on Mr Utterson, the reader knowing only what he knows, until the events leading up to Jekyll's death are revealed in his own and Dr Lanyon's narratives.
- The story told by Jonathan Small in *The Sign of Four* performs a similar function, fully explaining the mystery to the reader as well as to the narrator, Dr Watson.
- *The War of the Worlds* is told in chronological order and divided into two distinct 'books'. The narrator uses his brother's experiences, told in the third person, to report things he could not have seen.

The Narrative Voice

- Narrators in nineteenth-century novels use Standard English. However, narratives can be very different in tone. In a first-person narrative this can reflect the character of the protagonist. In other novels, we can still detect a distinctive authorial voice.

> **Key Point**
>
> Although all stories follow more or less the same structure (see page 36), novelists arrange their narratives in very different ways.

- Is your narrator's tone:
  - friendly?
  - **colloquial?**
  - **formal?**
  - **ironic?**
  - **authoritative?**
- As you are reading, do you feel the narrator is talking to you personally?
- In *A Christmas Carol* Dickens tells the story as if we were in a room with him.
- George Eliot frequently intervenes in the narrative. Some readers find her intrusions 'preachy'.
- Jane Austen's authorial voice is more detached – amused and ironic.

Speech

- Different characters can use language in different ways, adding to our understanding of them.
- They might:
  - use dialect or slang
  - use language in a comic way
  - have oddities or peculiarities of speech
  - use over-formal language
  - use language others might not understand.
- Magwitch's language, in *Great Expectations*, tells us a lot about him instantly. His pronunciation ('pint', 'wittles') places him in a different social class from Pip, and his cursing scares Pip.
- Sherlock Holmes uses technical terms to dazzle his listeners.

Descriptive Language

- Novelists use techniques in the same way as poets do to create mood and atmosphere. You might find that your novelist uses:
  - detail
  - varied sentence structures
  - alliteration, assonance and onomatopoeia
  - imagery
  - symbolism.
- Stevenson uses detail to build a vivid picture of Soho, where Hyde lives.
- In *Jane Eyre*, Brontë's description of the chestnut tree is hugely **symbolic**.

> **Key Point**
>
> The question in the exam will include a short extract from your novel. You should analyse the language used in it in detail.

> **Quick Test**
>
> What is meant by the following terms?
> 1. Dialect
> 2. Colloquial
> 3. Symbol
> 4. Flashback

> **Key Words**
>
> tone
> colloquial
> formal
> ironic
> authoritative
> symbolic

Answer the question on the play you have studied.

You should spend between 20 and 30 minutes on your answer. Write your answer on a separate piece of paper.

1 *Julius Caesar* – Read the extract specified and answer the question below.

In this extract, Cassius is trying to persuade Brutus to join him in conspiring against Caesar.

> **Act 1 Scene 2** *Read lines 130–144, from*
>
> CASSIUS   Ye gods, it doth amaze me
>
>   A man of such a feeble temper should
>
>   So get the start of the majestic world
>
>   And bear the palm alone.
>
> *To*
>
>   Brutus and Caesar: what should be in that 'Caesar'?
>
>   Why should that name be sounded more than yours?

Explore how Shakespeare presents the attitude of Cassius to Caesar in this extract.

Refer closely to the extract in your answer. [20]

2 *Much Ado About Nothing* – Read the extract specified and answer the question below.

In this extract, the marriage between Hero and Claudio has just been arranged.

> **Act 2 Scene 1** *Read lines 298–314, from*
>
> BEATRICE   Good Lord, for alliance! Thus goes everyone to the world but I, and I am sunburnt. I may sit in a corner and cry, 'Heigh-ho for a husband!'
>
> *To*
>
> BEATRICE   No, sure, my lord, my mother cried. But then there was a star danced, and under that was I born.

How does Shakespeare present Beatrice in this extract?

Refer closely to the extract in your answer. [20]

3 *The Merchant of Venice* – Read the extract specified and answer the question below.

In this extract, Tubal has brought Shylock news about his daughter, who has eloped with Lorenzo.

Act 3 Scene 1 *Read lines 100–114, from*

TUBAL   Your daughter spent in Genoa, as I heard, one night fourscore ducats.

To

SHYLOCK   Out upon her! Thou torturest me, Tubal. It was my turquoise; I had it of Leah when I was a bachelor. I would not have given it for a wilderness of monkeys.

Explore how Shakespeare presents Shylock's relationship with Jessica in this extract.

Refer closely to the extract in your answer. [20]

4   *Othello* – Read the extract specified and answer the question below.

In this extract, Othello has just married Desdemona against her father's wishes. He is about to leave for Cyprus and asks the Duke to find her somewhere to live.

Act 1 Scene 3 *Read lines 234–259, from*

OTHELLO   Most humbly, therefore, bending to your state,

                I crave fit disposition for my wife,

To

DESDEMONA   And I a heavy interim shall support

                By his dear absence. Let me go with him.

Look at the way Desdemona and Othello speak and behave here. What does it reveal to an audience about their relationship?

Refer closely to the extract in your answer. [20]

5   *Romeo and Juliet*

Explore how Shakespeare presents the growing love of Romeo and Juliet.

Write about the whole of the play. [20]

6   *Macbeth*

How does Shakespeare present Macbeth's feelings about power and ambition?

Write about the whole of the play. [20]

7   *The Tempest*

Write about how Shakespeare presents Ariel as a spirit and a slave.

Write about the whole of the play. [20]

8   *Twelfth Night*

Explore how Sir Toby Belch and Maria influence the events of the play and the reaction of the audience.

Write about the whole of the play. [20]

9   *Henry V*

Write about how ideas about kingship are presented in *Henry V*.

Write about the whole of the play. [20]

Answer the question on the novel you have studied.

You should spend between 20 and 30 minutes on your answer.

1 **Robert Louis Stevenson:** *The Strange Case of Dr Jekyll and Mr Hyde*

In this extract, the murder of Sir Danvers Carew has been witnessed by a maid.

Read Chapter 4

From

> When they had come within speech (which was just under the maid's eyes) the older man bowed and accosted the other with a very pretty manner of politeness.

To

> And next moment, with ape-like fury, he was trampling his victim under foot and hailing down a storm of blows, under which the bones were audibly shattered and the body jumped upon the roadway.

In this extract, how does Stevenson convey a sense of horror? Write about:

- the sense of horror conveyed in the extract
- how he uses language, structure and form to convey a sense of horror in the extract. **[20]**

2 **Charles Dickens:** *A Christmas Carol*

In this extract, two gentlemen have asked Scrooge to make a contribution to charity to help the poor.

Read Stave (Chapter) 1

From

> 'Are there no prisons?' asked Scrooge.

To

> 'It's not my business', Scrooge returned. 'It's enough for a man to understand his own business, and not to interfere with other people's. Mine occupies me constantly. Good afternoon, gentlemen!'

In this extract how does Dickens present Scrooge's attitude to other people? Write about:

- Scrooge's attitude in the extract
- how Dickens uses language, structure and form to present Scrooge's attitude in the extract. **[20]**

3 **Jane Austen:** *Pride and Prejudice*

In this extract, Mr Darcy and his friend Mr Bingley are attending a ball at Meryton, where they meet the Bennet family.

Read Chapter 3

From

> Elizabeth Bennet had been obliged, by the scarcity of gentlemen, to sit down for two dances;

To

> 'You had better return to your partner and enjoy her smiles, for you are wasting your time with me'.

In this extract, how does Austen present Mr Darcy's 'pride'? Write about:

- the impression we get of Mr Darcy in the extract
- how Austen uses language, form and structure to present his pride in the extract. **[20]**

4 **Charles Dickens: *Great Expectations***

In this extract Pip has just arrived in London.

> **Read Chapter 1**
>
> *From*
>
> 'So you were never in London before?' said Mr Wemmick to me.
>
> *To*
>
> We had got to the top of Holborn Hill before I knew that it was merely a mechanical appearance, and that he was not smiling at all.

In this extract, how does Dickens present Pip's arrival in London? Write about:

- the impressions we get of London and Pip's feelings about it in the extract
- how Dickens uses language, form and structure to present Pip's arrival in London. [20]

5 **H. G. Wells: *The War of the Worlds***

In this extract the narrator sees the Martians' 'cylinder' for the first time.

> **Read Chapter 3**
>
> *From*
>
> I found a little crowd of perhaps twenty people surrounding the huge hole in which the cylinder lay.
>
> *To*
>
> 'Extra-terrestrial' had no meaning for most of the onlookers.

In this extract, how does Wells present the reactions of humans to the arrival of the Martians? Write about:

- the reactions of the narrator and others to the cylinder, in the extract
- how Wells uses language, form and structure to present these reactions. [20]

6 **Mary Shelley: *Frankenstein***

How does Shelley present Frankenstein's feelings about his creation?

Write about the whole novel. Write about:

- Frankenstein's feelings about the monster
- the methods Shelley uses to present Frankenstein's feelings about the monster. [20]

7 **Sir Arthur Conan Doyle: *The Sign of Four***

Write about how Conan Doyle presents Sherlock Holmes as a great detective.

Write about the whole novel. Write about:

- what makes Holmes a great detective
- the methods Conan Doyle uses to present Holmes in the novel as a whole. [20]

8 **Charlotte Brontë: *Jane Eyre***

Write about how Brontë presents Jane's feelings for Mr Rochester.

Write about the whole novel. Write about:

- Jane's changing feelings about Rochester
- the methods Brontë uses to convey Jane's feelings towards him. [20]

9 **George Eliot: *Silas Marner***

Write about the character and significance of Godfrey Cass in *Silas Marner*.

Write about the whole novel. Write about:

- what Godfrey Cass does in the novel and what Eliot says about him
- the methods Eliot uses to present Godfrey Cass. [20]

Context

You must be able to:

- Understand the social, historical and cultural context of a modern text
- Use this understanding to evaluate the text.

Context

- You need to consider the social and historical context of your text. Think about the kind of society presented in the text.
- Think about 'cultural context', including genre and intended audience.

Time

- Your set text may have been written at any point in the last 100 years. Society has changed a lot in that time.
- The Britain portrayed in the set texts ranges from the hypocritical, class-conscious world of 1912 shown in *An Inspector Calls* to the violent, morally confused twenty-first-century world shown in *Pigeon English* and *DNA*.
- *An Inspector Calls*, written in 1945, looks back on an earlier **period**. This is 1912 seen from the perspective of a country that had experienced two world wars and in which many were looking forward to a new, fairer society. Someone writing in 1912 would have seen things differently.
- Other texts set in earlier periods include:
  - *The History Boys* (written in 2004, set in 1980s)
  - *Anita and Me* (written in 1996, set in 1960s/1970s)
  - *Hobson's Choice* (written in 1916, set in 1880)

  If you have studied a text set in the past, think about why the writer has chosen the period and how his or her view of it is coloured by the events, ideas and attitudes of later years.
- *Animal Farm* (1945) and *Lord of the Flies* (1954) are not set at a particular time but they are the product of their time. *Animal Farm* is based on the Russian Revolution of 1917 and written at a time of great concern about totalitarianism. *Lord of the Flies* picks up on post-war concerns about what is meant by civilization.
- Other texts – from *A Taste of Honey* (1956) to *Pigeon English* (2011) – reflect the world at the time they were written.

Key Point

Think about how your text reflects the concerns, attitudes and assumptions of the time and how these might differ from those of today.

Place

- The place where a text is set can help to give it a distinctive tone and atmosphere.
- Regional differences come out most strongly in the way characters speak:
  - Meera Syal presents the way people from a Black Country village speak by writing their speech phonetically, imitating the way they pronounce words.

- Helen in *A Taste of Honey* uses dialect expressions, such as 'I'd sooner be put on't street', reflecting the play's Lancashire setting.
- Some texts establish a sense of place by referring to specific **locations**:
  - *Blood Brothers* references places in and around Liverpool. The family's move from the city to a 'new town' marks the end of Act 1.
- Factors such as whether the setting is urban or rural, in the inner city or the suburbs, can be more important than the exact location:
  - *An Inspector Calls* takes place in a 'large suburban house' in a fictional industrial city.
- Some texts are set within a particular community or communities:
  - *Anita and Me* is about two very different communities co-existing: the village of Tollington and Meena's 'family' of Indians, who visit her house.
  - *Oranges Are Not the Only Fruit* describes growing up within a strict church in a Lancashire town.

Cultural Context

- If you are studying a play, think about where and for whom it was/is performed.
  - *Blood Brothers* is a musical. In **musical theatre** characters use songs to express emotion and to move the story on.
  - *DNA* was written to be performed by and for young people.
- With prose, too, genre can be important:
  - *Never Let Me Go* is sometimes categorized as science fiction. It is about what could happen as a result of science.
  - *The Woman in Black* is a ghost story, employing the traditional conventions of the genre.
  - Golding has called *Lord of the Flies* a **fable**, and *Animal Farm* is subtitled 'A fairy story'. What are the implications of these descriptions?

Key Point

Think about whether the place where your text is set makes a difference and, if so, how.

Quick Test

True or False?
1. A text's setting can determine how characters speak.
2. Characters in musicals express emotion by singing.
3. Science fiction is about things that have really happened.
4. Some texts are set in imaginary places.

Key Words

period
location
musical theatre
fable

Themes

You must be able to:

- Identify themes in a modern text
- Write about how themes are presented.

Identifying Themes

- Think about:
  - what the writer is saying
  - what the text makes you think about.
- Try answering, in one sentence, the question, 'What is the text about?'

Lord of the Flies is about a group of boys stranded on an island.

- Ask yourself why the writer might want us to read about this situation and what it makes us think about. You are now moving from the situation to the themes. Try to come up with some new answers to the question, 'What is the text about?' You could make a spider diagram or a list:

- Some themes crop up again and again in the set texts. Here are some questions that might get you thinking about themes and ideas in your text.

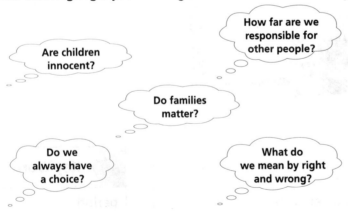

- Write down as many questions as you can that might come out of your text. Then try to find more than one answer to each, backing up your answer with evidence from the text.

> ### Key Point
>
> Themes in modern texts reflect current concerns, as well as issues that have always interested writers.

How Themes are Presented in Novels and Short Stories

Modern prose presents themes:
- through events:
  - In *Animal Farm*, a pig walks on its hind legs, showing that the pigs have become like the humans they replaced.
- through the narrator:
  - In *Anita and Me*, Meena draws lessons from her experiences about culture, friendship and growing up.
- through characters:
  - Steve in 'My Polish Teacher's Tie' represents identity and new possibilities to Carla.
- through what characters say:
  - In *Lord of the Flies*, the boys discuss issues like responsibility and survival.
- through motifs and symbols:
  - In 'The Odour of Chrysanthemums', the chrysanthemums are **ambiguous**. They represent unhappiness and death to Elizabeth, but she also associates them with happy memories.

How Themes are Presented in Plays

- The stage is a visual **medium**. It is about showing, not telling. Look in the stage directions for striking **images** which encapsulate themes:
  - The image of Mickey and Edward lying dead at the end of *Blood Brothers* brings together many of the play's themes.

  Remember, though, that play **scripts** can be interpreted differently by different **directors**, designers and actors. The images of one production may not be the same as those of another.
- Characters sometimes speak directly to the audience, bringing our attention to themes and issues:
  - In *The History Boys*, Scripps occasionally steps out of the action to reflect on the meaning of the boys' experiences.
- Mostly, we encounter themes and ideas through dialogue. There can be as many different points of view about an issue as there are characters on stage:
  - In *DNA* different ideas about guilt and honesty emerge as the characters discuss their actions.
- Some writers present us with several **viewpoints** and leave us to make up our own minds. Others give their preferred point of view to a character who is presented as being wiser or more trustworthy than others:
  - Inspector Goole in *An Inspector Calls* stands apart from the action, and his **interpretation** of what has happened can be seen as that of the writer.

> ### Key Point
>
> Our interpretation of themes and ideas can depend as much on our background and opinions as on those of the writer.

> ### Key Words
>
> diagram
> prose
> ambiguous
> medium
> image
> script
> director
> viewpoint
> interpretation

Quick Test

In the theatre, which of the following influence how themes are presented?
1. The writer.
2. The director.
3. The actors.
4. The designer.

Characters

You must be able to:

- Write about how characters are presented in a modern text.

Prose: First-Person Narratives

- *Never Let Me Go, Anita and Me, The Woman in Black, Oranges Are Not the Only Fruit* and *Pigeon English* are first-person narratives.
- Kathy in *Never Let Me Go* and Meena in *Anita and Me* write as adults looking back on their past. Harrison in *Pigeon English* tells us the story as it happens, like a diary.
- Adult narrators usually have a greater understanding of their stories. Arthur Kipps in *The Woman in Black* is as mystified as the reader by the events he witnesses but reflects on what they might mean.
- We can get an idea of what other characters think of the narrator, but this is always filtered through the narrator's perspective:
  - In *Never Let Me Go* Kathy does not always understand how others are responding to her, but the reader can make inferences from what she reports.
- Readers might draw conclusions about narrators which the narrators (and possibly writers) do not foresee:
  - Some readers might think Meena in *Anita and Me* comes across as a snob who looks down on her old friends.
- We might draw our own conclusions, different from those of the narrator, about other characters:
  - The narrator in 'Chemistry' is **naive** and his naivety makes him **unreliable**. At the end his assessment of other characters is called into question.

Prose: Third-Person Narratives

- Although it is a third-person narrative, the action in 'The Darkness Out There' is seen through the eyes of Sandra, so we learn about her thoughts and feelings. Similarly, in 'The Odour of Chrysanthemums' we share Elizabeth's thoughts.
- Golding is an **omniscient** narrator in *Lord of the Flies*. The character we are given most insight into is the protagonist, Ralph, but he also takes us into the minds of other characters.
- In *Lord of the Flies* there is a strong antagonist in Jack. Other characters, like Piggy and Simon, are important because of what they do in the story and because of what they represent.
- The characters in *Animal Farm* are different from conventional characters. Most of them are animals, which fits with the novel being called a 'fairy tale' or 'fable'. Some of them can be identified with real historical figures, such as Lenin and Trotsky, but they can also be seen as 'types': for example, the honest worker, the spy, the tyrant.

 Key Point

Modern novelists tell us about characters in the same ways as nineteenth-century novelists did.

Drama

- Sometimes **playwrights** tell us about characters in stage directions:
  - Arthur Birling in *An Inspector Calls* is described as 'a heavy-looking, rather portentous man in his middle fifties, with fairly easy manners but rather provincial in his speech'.
- Characters can reveal themselves, either directly to the audience or to other characters. Judy in *The Curious Incident of the Dog in the Night-Time* gives her side of things through letters:

> And your father is really patient, but I'm not. I get cross, even though I don't mean to [...] and I felt really lonely.

- We learn about characters through dialogue. When Dakin and Scripps converse in *The History Boys* we hear their differing points of view, and we see that they are both intellectually, if not emotionally, mature as they can express themselves well, using sophisticated diction:

> No more the bike's melancholy long withdrawing roar as he dropped you off at the corner, your honour still intact.

- What really matters is what characters do:
  - Mrs Johnstone in *Blood Brothers* gives away one of her children. Why? And what are the consequences?
  - In *Hobson's Choice*, Maggie proposes to Willie and then insists on having a brass wedding ring 'out of stock'.

Quick Test

Rearrange the letters to find a useful term:
1. TSGNROAPTOI
2. RRRTNAOA
3. GIDOULEA
4. GATES TIRODENIC

Language and Structure

You must be able to:

- Analyse the use of language and structure in a modern text
- Use relevant terminology.

Prose

The Narrative Voice

- In *Pigeon English* the narrator appears to be speaking to the reader. Because of his age and background, he does not use Standard English. His use of dialect and slang ('donkey hours', 'hutious') gives a sense of where he lives and where he comes from.
- Some narrators, like Kathy in *Never Let Me Go*, adopt a colloquial tone while using Standard English, as if explaining things to a friend:

> I suppose that might sound odd.

- Others, like the boy in 'Chemistry', write about their lives in a more detached, adult way, also using Standard English.

Speech

- The language characters use adds to our understanding of them and the world they inhabit.
- Most of the boys in *Lord of the Flies* speak in Standard English, but in the rather clipped manner of public schoolboys in the 1950s:

> 'Give him a fourpenny one!'

Piggy is shown to be from a different class:

> 'I got the conch, ain't I Ralph?'

- In *Anita and Me*, the local people use dialect and their **accent** is shown phonetically:

> 'Ay up, Mr K! Havin a bit of a do then?'

The Indian characters use Standard English except when speaking Punjabi.

Structure

- Most of the set texts are written in chronological order, although some of them (*Anita and Me*, *Never Let Me Go*) jump backwards and forwards as one event reminds the narrator of another.
- Think about how the text is divided. Why does the writer decide to start a new chapter at a certain point?

> **Key Point**
>
> In first-person narratives, the language of the narration can reflect the background of the narrator.

- Look for anything different or odd about your text's structure:
  - Some sections of *Pigeon English* start with the pigeon narrating, distinguished from the rest of the text by being in italics.
  - Jeanette Winterson in *Oranges Are Not the Only Fruit* uses the titles of books of the Old Testament for her chapters.

Drama

Language

- **Dialogue** can reflect where the play is set and also tell us about the characters.
- The class divisions of *Blood Brothers* are shown in the contrast between the way the Johnstone and Lyons families speak:

> EDWARD: Do you…Do you really? Goodness, that's fantastic.

> MICKEY: Come on, bunk under y'fence, y'Ma won't see y'.

- Christopher in *The Curious Incident of the Dog in the Night-Time* speaks in a deliberate, rather impersonal way:

> I remember 20 July 2006. I was 9 years old. It was a Saturday.

Structure

- Most plays are in two **acts**, with an **interval** between them. Because of this, writers usually build up to a **turning point** at the end of Act 1, leaving the audience wanting to know what happens next.
- When *An Inspector Calls* was written, most plays had a three-act structure, so both Act 1 and Act 2 end with turning points.
- *An Inspector Calls*, *Journey's End* and *A Taste of Honey* have clear act and **scene** divisions. Within each section, action is continuous and happens in one place.
- In other, more recent plays the action flows from one short scene to another, time and place changing frequently.
- Look for anything unusual about your play's structure, for example:
  - At the end of *An Inspector Calls*, it looks as though the play is about to start all over again.
  - In *The History Boys* characters seem to jump out of the 'past' to speak to us and then return seamlessly.
  - The story of the women in *My Mother Said I Never Should* is structured in short scenes, arranged in chronological order, but these are punctuated by the 'wasteland' scenes where all the women play together as little girls.

 Key Point

When we discuss language in a play we are discussing the language the characters use.

Quick Test

1. Can a narrator use a colloquial tone and Standard English?
2. In the same play, which is longer, a scene or an act?
3. What would the use of dialect tell us about a character?
4. Are the events in a play or novel always in chronological order?

 Key Words

accent
dialogue
act
interval
turning point
scene

Answer the question on the novel you have studied.

Spend between 20 and 30 minutes on your answer.

1 **Mary Shelley:** *Frankenstein*

In this extract, Victor Frankenstein describes seeing the monster he has created.

Read Chapter 5

From

It was on a dreary night of November that I beheld the accomplishment of my toils.

To

…but these luxuriances only formed a more horrid contrast with his watery eyes, that seemed almost of the same colour as the dun white sockets in which they were set, his shrivelled complexion and straight black lips.

In this extract, how does Shelley present Frankenstein's feelings about his creation? Write about:

* Frankenstein's reaction to the monster in this extract
* how Shelley uses language, form and structure to convey Frankenstein's feelings about the monster in this extract. **[20]**

2 **Sir Arthur Conan Doyle:** *The Sign of Four*

In this extract, Holmes and Watson are searching Pondicherry House for clues about the murder of Bartholomew Sholto.

Read Chapter 6

From

He held down the lamp to the floor, and as he did so I saw for the second time that night a startled, surprised look come over his face.

To

'What then?' I asked.

'Why, we have got him, that's all', said he.

In this extract, how does Conan Doyle present Sherlock Holmes as a great detective? Write about:
* what Sherlock Holmes does and says in this extract
* how Conan Doyle uses language, form and structure to present Holmes as a great detective in this extract. **[20]**

3 **Charlotte Brontë:** *Jane Eyre*

In this extract, Jane meets Mr Rochester for the first time.

Read Chapter 12

From

I was in the mood for being useful, or at least officious, I think, for I now drew near him again.

To

He looked at me when I said this; he had hardly turned his eyes in my direction before.

In this extract, how does Brontë present Jane's feelings about Mr Rochester? Write about:
- how Jane describes and reacts to Rochester in this extract
- how Brontë uses language, structure and form to convey Jane's feelings towards Rochester in this extract.

[20]

4   **George Eliot:** *Silas Marner*

In this extract, Dunstan Cass threatens to tell his father about his brother's secret marriage.

> **Read Chapter 3**
>
> *From*
>> The door opened, and a thick-set, heavy-looking young man entered, with the flushed face and the gratuitously elated bearing which mark the first stage of intoxication.
>
> *To*
>> 'You'll get the hundred pounds for me – I know you will.'

In this extract, how does Eliot present the Cass family? Write about:
- how Godfrey and Duncan behave and speak in this extract
- how Eliot uses language, structure and form to convey their characters and relationship.

[20]

5   **Robert Louis Stevenson:** *The Strange Case of Dr Jekyll and Mr Hyde*

How does Stevenson convey an atmosphere of mystery and horror?
Write about the whole novel. Write about:
- the atmosphere of mystery and horror in the novel
- the methods Stevenson uses to convey an atmosphere of mystery and horror.

[20]

6   **Charles Dickens:** *A Christmas Carol*

How does Dickens present Scrooge's attitude to other people?
Write about the whole novel. Write about:
- Scrooge's attitude to other people
- how Dickens presents Scrooge's attitude.

[20]

7   **Jane Austen:** *Pride and Prejudice*

How does Austen present Mr Darcy's 'pride'?
Write about the whole novel. Write about:
- to what extent and in what ways Darcy is proud
- the methods Austen uses to present his 'pride'.

[20]

8   **Charles Dickens:** *Great Expectations*

Write about how Dickens presents Pip's journey into adulthood.
Write about the whole novel. Write about:
- the stages in Pip's journey into adulthood
- the methods Dickens uses to present Pip's journey into adulthood.

[20]

9   **H. G. Wells:** *The War of the Worlds*

Write about how Wells presents ideas about how fear affects human beings.
Write about the whole novel. Write about:
- how fear affects people in different parts of the novel
- the methods Wells uses to present the effects of fear.

[20]

Answer the question on the text or texts you have studied.

Your answer should be in note form, using bullet points.

In your answer, write down five statements about the character and give evidence from the text in support of each one.

1 **J. B. Priestley: *An Inspector Calls***

Make notes on the character and significance of Inspector Goole in *An Inspector Calls*.   [10]

2 **Willy Russell: *Blood Brothers***

Make notes on the character and significance of Mrs Lyons in *Blood Brothers*.   [10]

3 **Alan Bennett: *The History Boys***

Make notes on the character and significance of Dakin in *The History Boys*.   [10]

4 **Dennis Kelly: *DNA***

Make notes on the character and significance of Leah in *DNA*.   [10]

5 **Simon Stephens: *The Curious Incident of the Dog in the Night-Time***

Make notes on the character and significance of Christopher in *The Curious Incident of the Dog in the Night-Time*.   [10]

6 **Shelagh Delaney: *A Taste of Honey***

Make notes on the character and significance of Jo in *A Taste of Honey*.   [10]

7 **Harold Brighouse: *Hobson's Choice***

Make notes on the character and significance of Willie Mossop in *Hobson's Choice*.   [10]

8 **R. C. Sherriff: *Journey's End***

Make notes on the character and significance of Stanhope in *Journey's End*.   [10]

9 **Charlotte Keatley: *My Mother Said I Never Should***

Make notes on the character and significance of Margaret in *My Mother Said I Never Should*.   [10]

10 **William Golding: *Lord of the Flies***

Make notes on the character and significance of Simon in *Lord of the Flies*.   [10]

11 **AQA Anthology: *Telling Tales***

Make notes on the character and significance of Carla in 'My Polish Teacher's Tie'.   [10]

12 **George Orwell: *Animal Farm***

Make notes on the character and significance of Boxer in *Animal Farm*. [10]

13 **Kazuo Ishiguro: *Never Let Me Go***

Make notes on the character and significance of Tommy in *Never Let Me Go*. [10]

14 **Meera Syal: *Anita and Me***

Make notes on the character and significance of Anita in *Anita and Me*. [10]

15 **Stephen Kelman: *Pigeon English***

Make notes on the character and significance of Harrison in *Pigeon English*. [10]

16 **Susan Hill: *The Woman in Black***

Make notes on the character and significance of Arthur Kipps in *The Woman in Black*. [10]

17 **Jeanette Winterson: *Oranges Are Not the Only Fruit***

Make notes on the character and significance of Jeanette's mother in *Oranges Are Not the Only Fruit*. [10]

Context

You must be able to:

- Understand the social, historical and cultural context of poetry
- Use this understanding in your evaluation of texts.

Time and Place

- Many poems focus on personal memories, and the poets evoke a sense of the time and place they are remembering:
  - In 'In Paris With You' James Fenton remembers tiny details about the hotel in Paris. He draws on the associations of the city with romance, and the phrase 'in Paris' becomes a substitute for 'in love'.
  - In 'Eden Rock' Charles Causley freezes his parents in time, with references to their clothes and their picnic (Thermos, HP Sauce bottle), although he ends by teasing the reader with his assertion that the place is made up.
- Some poems are about historical events, and some knowledge and understanding of these events can be helpful:
  - 'Exposure' and 'Anthem for Doomed Youth' are both personal and historical as they are based around Owen's own experiences in the First World War. His reactions are personal and immediate.
  - Simon Armitage's poems 'Remains' and 'The Manhunt' are inspired by the experiences of soldiers who fought in the recent war in Iraq.
- The attitudes of the poets to their subjects should be seen in the context of their own time:
  - 'The Charge of the Light Brigade', inspired by a newspaper article, reflects popular sentiment at the time by criticizing the orders given to the Brigade but glorifying the soldiers themselves.
- When a poet writes about something in the past, consider both the time when it was written and the time it was written about.
  - Browning's **dramatic monologues** use historical settings to present characters that must have been shocking as well as fascinating to his huge Victorian readership, reflecting an interest in psychology.
  - 'Kamikaze' presents the attitudes of Japanese people in the Second World War to a modern audience.

> ### Key Point
>
> When comparing poems from the anthology, you must think about similarities and differences between their contexts.

The Romantic Movement

- Blake, Byron, Shelley and Wordsworth were all part of the Romantic **movement** in literature. An understanding of Romanticism will inform your reading of their poetry.
- In the eighteenth century most English poets admired and imitated Greek and Latin poetry. Intellectuals valued logic and reason above feelings.
- The Romantics rebelled against this. They used more traditional forms of poetry, such as the **ballad**, using simpler rhythms and rhyme

schemes and more everyday language. They sometimes wrote about ordinary people.

- Most of their poetry, whether lyric poetry (short poems about feelings) like 'Love's Philosophy' or the lengthy autobiographical 'Prelude', focuses on emotions, which they often associated with nature.
- They could also be political, inspired by events like the French Revolution to write anti-establishment poems like 'London'.
- Later poets continued to be influenced by the Romantics. You can see this in Hardy, the Brontës and Mew, and modern poets like Sheers and Hughes.

Social Issues

- Gender can be important in poems:
  - The relationship between the farmer and his bride in Charlotte Mew's poem seems to have more to do with power than love. The traditional roles the man and woman are given create misery for both.
  - To the Duke in 'My Last Duchess', his wife is just a possession.
- Ideas about cultural identity are central to 'Checking Out Me History'. The poet is angry about being given a 'white' version of history when growing up in the British Empire.
- 'London' is concerned with the poverty, disease and inequality of its time.

Key Point

'Context' refers to literary traditions and movements as well as to social and historical influences.

Quick Test

True or False?
1. Romantic poets were not political.
2. When a poem is set does not matter.
3. Wordsworth is a Romantic poet.
4. Lyric poetry is about feelings.

Key Words

dramatic monologue
movement
ballad
lyric

Themes

You must be able to:

- Identify themes in poetry
- Compare how themes are presented.

Themes and Ideas in the Anthology

- The poems in your anthology may have been grouped together under broad themes, such as 'Time and Place' and 'Love and Relationships'.
- If so, consider what aspect of the main theme the poet is writing about.
- Look for other themes, ideas and issues that might be present.
- Consider the poet's attitudes to these themes.
- Connect the poems through their treatment of themes, looking for both similarities and differences.

How Themes are Presented in Poetry

- Poems often focus on an incident or moment in life, perhaps an anecdote or a snapshot of someone's feelings at a certain time.
- Some poems, like Browning's 'My Last Duchess' and Clarke's 'Cold Knap Lake', tell a story. 'Cold Knap Lake' tells a story and then reflects on its meaning, as does 'The Charge of the Light Brigade'. 'My Last Duchess', on the other hand, does not include the poet's thoughts, leaving readers to infer meaning.
- Many poems have no story but tell us directly about the poet's thoughts and feelings. Some poets express strong views and feelings, as in Agard's 'Flag' and 'Half-caste' and Barrett Browning's sonnets.
- Others, like 'Neutral Tones' and 'Adlestrop', present us with images and experiences, leaving us to infer the poet's attitudes and feelings.
- At times it is impossible to 'work out' what the poet's feelings are, as the poem is ambiguous. The poet might not have the answer or might want readers to come up with their own answers.

> **Key Point**
>
> The same poem can mean different things to different people. Your response and interpretation is as valid as anyone else's – and it is your response that the examiner wants to read.

Connections

- In your exam you are required to write about two poems that you have studied. Here are some questions you could ask when comparing poems during revision.

Love and Relationships

- What sort of relationship is it?

(Lovers) (Husband and wife) (Parents and children) (Other family relationships)

- What else is the poem about?

(Time passing) (Culture and identity) (Death) (Betrayal) (Hope) (Power)

- What feelings does the **voice** or **persona** in the poem have about the subject of the poem?

> Love   Jealousy   Indifference   Obsession   Anger

What is the attitude of the subject to the voice/persona?

Power and Conflict

- What kind of conflict is it?

> An argument   A war   A psychological conflict

- What kind of power is it?

> The power of a government or state   The power of an individual   Physical power   Mental power

- Or is it about lack of power?
- What else is the poem about?

> Loss   Death   Love   Nature   Memory

- What does the poet feel about the subject of the poem?

> Anger   Sorrow   Fear   Disgust   Regret   Confusion

Time and Place

- Where is the poem set?

> In the recent past   In history   Spring, summer, autumn or winter   At a particular time of day   On a special occasion

- Where is it set?

> Somewhere the poet knows well   A strange or foreign place   An imagined place

- How does the poet feel about the place and/or time?

> Nostalgic   Regretful   Inspired   Intrigued

Youth and Age

- Who is in the poem?

> Children or young people   Older people

- What does the poet feel about the subject?

> Love   Regret   Dislike

- What else is the poem about?

> Parents and children   How society treats the old / the young   Growing up / growing old   Death   Innocence and experience

> **Key Point**
>
> You will also need to think about and comment on themes and ideas when writing about unseen poetry.

Quick Test

1. Can a poem be about conflict and relationships?
2. Can the title of the cluster help you think about themes?
3. Should you write about your response to the poems?
4. Will you always know what the poet's feelings are?

> **Key Words**
>
> attitude
> ambiguous
> voice
> persona

Language

You must be able to:

- Analyse poets' use of language, using appropriate terminology
- Compare how poets use language.

Sound

- Look at the ways poets use sound. Read the poems out loud or listen to someone else reading them.
- The most obvious way in which sound reflects meaning is through **onomatopoeia**:
  - Elizabeth Barrett Browning uses the phrase 'rustle thy boughs' to convey the sound of the wind in the trees (Sonnet 29).
- **Alliteration** can convey different moods, according to the sound used:
  - In 'Kamikaze' Beatrice Garland uses 's' sounds (also known as sibilance) to reflect the peaceful mood, as she describes fish 'flashing silver as their bellies swivelled toward the sun'.
  - Browning uses plosive sounds to sinister effect, almost as if he were spitting, in 'Porphyria's Lover':

> Blushed bright beneath my burning kiss.

- **Assonance** is the use of a series of similar vowel sounds to create patterns and atmosphere:

> but as we moved on through the afternoon light ('Winter Swans')

- Poets often repeat not just sounds, but whole words and phrases, emphasizing their importance, as in Agard's 'Flag':

> It's just a piece of cloth.

Or reflecting the repetition of an action and its impact, as in 'The Charge of the Light Brigade':

> Cannon to the right of them.
> Cannon to the left of them.

- A phrase which is repeated at the end of each stanza is often called a **refrain**.

Diction

- When poets use a **persona**, their choice of words helps to create the character. Browning, in 'My Last Duchess', uses colloquial language to make it seem as if the persona is having a conversation:

> A heart – how shall I say? – too soon made glad

> **Key Point**
>
> The poet Coleridge defined poetry as 'the best words in the best order'. Poets choose their words carefully.

- In 'Singh Song!' Daljit Nagra changes the spelling of words to reflect his persona's accent:

> But ven nobody in, I do di lock.

- In 'Checking Out Me History', John Agard speaks as himself but he uses the dialect of his childhood to convey both character and situation:

> Dem tell me bout de man who discover de balloon

- Other poets use specialized or technical vocabulary to give us a sense of a character, as Seamus Heaney does in 'Follower':

> He would set the wing
> And fit the bright steel-pointed sock.

- You might see self-consciously 'poetic' or even **archaic** (outdated) words used for effect, as in Barrett Browning's use of 'thee' rather than 'you'.

Imagery

- Imagery is central to our understanding of how poets create meaning. When a poet compares something to something else, think about why that comparison has been made.
- In 'The Farmer's Bride' Charlotte Mew's persona uses a series of **similes** to describe his bride:

> Straight and slight as a young larch tree,
> Sweet as the first wild violets, she.

- In 'Winter Swans' Owen Sheers uses the **metaphor** of 'porcelain' to convey the fragility and beauty of the swans.
- In 'Love's Philosophy' Shelley uses pathetic fallacy, personifying nature:

> See the mountains kiss high heaven.

- In 'Ozymandias' his description of the statue can be read as a **symbol** of the futility of power and the passing of time.

> **Key Point**
>
> Think about the 'voice' in the poem. Is the poet writing as him/herself or as a character – a 'persona'?

He compares her to things that he, as a farmer, would be familiar with, and he describes her as a wild thing, part of nature.

> **Key Words**
>
> onomatopoeia
> alliteration
> assonance
> refrain
> persona
> archaic
> simile
> metaphor
> symbol

> **Quick Test**
>
> Give the correct term for:
> 1. The use of a word that sounds like what it describes.
> 2. Writing about a thing or idea as if it were a person.
> 3. Starting a series of words with the same sound.
> 4. A character in a poem who speaks in the first person.

Form and Structure

You must be able to:

- Analyse poets' use of form and structure, using appropriate terminology
- Compare how poets use form and structure.

Stanzas

- Look at how many **stanzas** there are and whether they are equal in length.
- Hardy's 'Neutral Tones' is divided into four stanzas of four lines each. This is the traditional form of the ballad, a poem that tells a story. It is about strong feelings, so you might expect the poet to lose control. Instead he imposes order on his emotions. What effect does the tension between form and content have on the reader?
- Other poets, like Tennyson in 'The Charge of the Light Brigade', vary the length of their stanzas. If this is the case, think about what is happening in the poem when a poet adds an extra line or includes a very short stanza.
- Think about when the poet starts a new stanza. Is there a new idea being introduced? Or is there a change in place or time?
- Where a poem is not divided into stanzas, think about why this might be. Browning's 'Porphyria's Lover' is a dramatic monologue, in which the poet gives the impression that the persona is speaking to us spontaneously. Perhaps he does not stop to think.
- Single-stanza poems can have their own internal structure. Sonnets, such as Elizabeth Barrett Browning's Sonnet 29 and Sonnet 43, follow strict rules, in this case those of the **Petrarchan sonnet**. These consist of an **octave** (8 lines) followed by a **sestet** (6 lines). Traditionally the change from the octave to the sestet reflects a turn (called the **volta**) or change in the argument or mood. **Shakespearean sonnets** consist of three **quatrains** followed by a rhyming couplet.
- If a line ends with a punctuation mark, it is called **end-stopping**. If a poet continues across lines or even stanzas without a pause, it is called **enjambment**. Think about why the poet would choose one or the other.

Rhyme

- Rhyme is easy to spot but can be difficult to comment on. It can be used to make us laugh, to emphasize something, or to give a sense of order.
- The simplest form of rhyme is the **rhyming couplet**, rhyming one line with the next. This is an almost childish use of rhyme, so when it is used in a poem like 'The Farmer's Bride' it could be telling us something about the persona.
- Rhyming couplets are also used to underline important points.

> **Key Point**
>
> 'Stanza' is Italian for 'room', so if a poem is a house the stanzas are its rooms.

- The traditional rhyme scheme of the ballad is *abab*. Blake uses this in 'London' and 'A Poison Tree'. Although 'Neutral Tones' has the shape of a ballad, the rhyme scheme is different.
- Some poets use more complex rhyme schemes, while others use rhyme occasionally for effect, sometimes within lines (internal rhyme).
- You might come across sight or eye rhymes, where the words look as if they should rhyme but do not, for example, 'rough' and 'bough'.
- Many poets use 'half rhyme' (also known as 'slant rhyme' and 'pararhyme'), where the final consonants agree but the vowel sounds do not match, softening the effect of the rhyme. Thomas rhymes 'despair' and 'clear' in 'The Sorrow of True Love'.

Rhythm

- A poem's **rhythm** comes from its pattern of **stressed** and unstressed **syllables**. You can get a sense of this by reading a poem aloud.
- Some poems have a very strong rhythm. 'The Charge of the Light Brigade' is written in dactyls (a stressed syllable followed by two unstressed syllables), giving a sense of the pounding of horses' hooves and cannons:

> **Half** a league **half** a league

- One of the most commonly used **metres** is the iambic pentameter. This is quite a gentle rhythm, often compared to a heartbeat. Wordsworth uses it in 'The Prelude':

> And **as I rose** up**on** the **stroke**, my **boat**

- Contemporary poets are less likely to use strong rhythmical patterns, though there are exceptions like 'Checking Out Me History'. However, if you listen carefully you should still hear a rhythm. If you do, think about how the poet uses it to create the mood and tone of the poem.
- Poetry that has a regular metre but no rhyme is called **blank verse**. Poetry that has no regular pattern, either of rhyme or metre, is called **free verse**.

> ### Key Point
>
> When looking at rhyme and metre, look for patterns and variations in patterns.

> ### Key Words
>
> stanza
> Petrarchan sonnet
> octave
> sestet
> volta
> Shakespearean sonnet
> quatrain
> end-stopping
> enjambment
> rhyme
> rhyming couplet
> rhythm
> stress
> syllable
> metre
> blank verse
> free verse

> ### Quick Test
>
> Give the correct term for:
> 1. A set of two lines that rhyme.
> 2. A rhyme within a line.
> 3. A poem that tells a story in four-line stanzas.
> 4. Poetry that has no regular pattern.

Unseen Poetry

You must be able to:

- Respond to and analyse a poem you have not seen before
- Compare two poems.

Approaching an Unseen Poem

- In your exam you will have to write about at least one poem that you have never seen before.
- Start by reading the poem to gain a general sense of its themes, mood and atmosphere. Then use your knowledge of poetry to 'interrogate' the text. Here are some questions you could ask yourself when reading an unseen poem.

Title	What does it make you think about?
	Does it tell you what the poem is about or is it ambiguous?
Speaker	Is the voice in the poem that of the poet or a persona?
	Who, if anyone, is being addressed?
Setting	Where and when is it set?
	Does the place change?
	Does the time change?
Form and structure	How is it arranged?
	When and why does the poet start a new stanza?
	Is there a strong regular rhythm? If so, what effect does it have?
	Does it rhyme? If so, is there a regular rhyme scheme? What is the effect of the rhyme?
Language	How does the poet use sound?
	What kind of vocabulary/register does the poet use?
	What sort of imagery does the poet use?
	Is there anything else interesting about the language?
Themes and ideas	Is there a story? If so, what is it?
	What do you think the poem is really about?
	Is more than one theme touched on?
	What do you think is the poet's attitude / point of view?
Personal response	What does the poem make you think about?
	How does it make you feel?

Key Point

To answer the questions, you will need all the skills you have learned studying poems from the anthology.

Comparing Unseen Poems

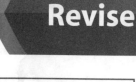

- If your question is in two parts and you are asked to write about one poem on its own before comparing it with another (AQA and WJEC), be careful not to repeat everything you have already said about the first poem. Focus on the second poem but make sure that every point you make refers back to the first one.
- You could go through the new poem line by line, linking it to the first poem as you go.
- Or you could take different aspects of the poem in turn, starting a new paragraph for each.
- If you are just asked to compare two poems (Edexcel and OCR), the best approach is to take different aspects of the poem in turn, making sure that you refer to both poems in every paragraph.
- Whichever way you approach the comparison, consider:

Structure and form	Brown's structure is regular, the four stanzas of four lines giving a sense of order and logic, whereas Smith's stanzas vary in length, as if her memories are random and disordered.
Language	Brown's use of harsh-sounding words such as 'rough' and 'dour' contrast with the softness of Smith's 'silken voice' and 'shuffling step'.
Imagery	Both poets use imagery connected with nature but in very different ways...
How the poets approach the theme	Both poems focus on the child's relationship with her father.
The poets' feelings and attitude	Unlike Brown, Smith remembers her father with affection.
Your response to the poems	Brown conveys a sense of regret and anger, whereas the way Smith describes her feelings, although sad, is somehow comforting.

- Back up every point you make with short quotations from both poems.
- Try to use correct **terminology** but remember that you do not get marks just for 'spotting' things like alliteration and metaphors. You must show that you understand how they are used and their effect on the reader.

> ### Key Point
>
> If you are doing the OCR exam you will be required to compare an unseen poem with a poem from the anthology. The other boards will give you two unseen poems to compare.

> ## Quick Test
>
> Would you use the following connectives to express a similarity or a difference?
> 1. Both...and
> 2. whereas...
> 3. On the other hand...
> 4. Neither...nor

> ### Key Word
>
> terminology

Answer the question on the text you have studied.

Your answer should be in note form, using bullet points.

In your answer, write down five statements and give evidence from the text in support of each one.

1 **J. B. Priestley:** *An Inspector Calls*

How does Priestley write about attitudes to women in *An Inspector Calls*? [10]

2 **Willy Russell:** *Blood Brothers*

How does Russell write about fate in *Blood Brothers*? [10]

3 **Alan Bennett:** *The History Boys*

How does Bennett write about history in *The History Boys*? [10]

4 **Dennis Kelly:** *DNA*

How does Kelly write about guilt and responsibility in *DNA*? [10]

5 **Simon Stephens:** *The Curious Incident of the Dog in the Night-Time*

How does Stephens explore ideas about families in *The Curious Incident of the Dog in the Night-Time*? [10]

6 **Shelagh Delaney:** *A Taste of Honey*

How does Delaney present ideas about love in *A Taste of Honey*? [10]

7 **Harold Brighouse:** *Hobson's Choice*

How does Brighouse write about courtship and marriage in *Hobson's Choice*? [10]

8 **R. C. Sherriff:** *Journey's End*

How does Sherriff write about fear in *Journey's End*? [10]

9 **Charlotte Keatley:** *My Mother Said I Never Should*

How does Keatley write about being a mother in *My Mother Said I Never Should*? [10]

10 **William Golding:** *Lord of the Flies*

How does Golding explore ideas about civilization in *Lord of the Flies*? [10]

11 **AQA Anthology:** *Telling Tales*

How does Lawrence write about death in 'The Odour of Chrysanthemums'? [10]

12 **George Orwell: *Animal Farm***

How does Orwell present ideas about oppression in *Animal Farm*? [10]

13 **Kazuo Ishiguro: *Never Let Me Go***

How does Ishiguro write about friendship in *Never Let Me Go*? [10]

14 **Meera Syal: *Anita and Me***

How does Syal write about living in two cultures in *Anita and Me*? [10]

15 **Stephen Kelman: *Pigeon English***

How does Kelman present ideas about violence in *Pigeon English*? [10]

16 **Susan Hill: *The Woman in Black***

How does Hill write about the supernatural in *The Woman in Black*? [10]

17 **Jeanette Winterson: *Oranges Are Not the Only Fruit***

How does Winterson explore ideas about belonging in *Oranges Are Not the Only Fruit*? [10]

Answer the question on the anthology and cluster you have studied. You will need a copy of the anthology.

Write your answers on a separate piece of paper.

1 **AQA Anthology: Power and Conflict**

Compare 'Kamikaze' with one other poem from 'Power and Conflict'. Write about:
* what the poems are about and what happens in them
* the poets' use of language
* the poets' use of form and structure
* the feelings and attitudes of the poets
* your response to the poems.

Refer closely to both poems. [20]

2 **AQA Anthology: Love and Relationships**

Compare 'Love's Philosophy' with one other poem from 'Love and Relationships'. Write about:
* what the poems are about and what happens in them
* the poets' use of language
* the poets' use of form and structure
* the feelings and attitudes of the poets
* your response to the poems.

Refer closely to both poems. [20]

3 **Edexcel Anthology: Relationships**

Compare Sonnet 43 with one other poem from 'Relationships'. Write about:
* what the poems are about and what happens in them
* the poets' use of language
* the poets' use of form and structure
* the feelings and attitudes of the poets
* your response to the poems.

Refer closely to both poems. [20]

4 **Edexcel Anthology: Conflict**

Compare 'Cousin Kate' with one other poem from 'Conflict'. Write about:
* what the poems are about and what happens in them
* the poets' use of language
* the poets' use of form and structure
* the feelings and attitudes of the poets
* your response to the poems.

Refer closely to both poems. [20]

5 **Edexcel Anthology: Time and Place**

Compare 'Adlestrop' with one other poem from 'Time and Place'. Write about:
* what the poems are about and what happens in them
* the poets' use of language

- the poets' use of form and structure
- the feelings and attitudes of the poets
- your response to the poems.

Refer closely to both poems. [20]

6 **OCR Anthology (*Towards a World Unknown*): Love and Relationships**

Compare 'Long Distance II' with one other poem from 'Love and Relationships'. Write about:
- what the poems are about and what happens in them
- the poets' use of language
- the poets' use of form and structure
- the feelings and attitudes of the poets
- your response to the poems.

Refer closely to both poems. [20]

7 **OCR Anthology (*Towards a World Unknown*): Conflict**

Compare 'Anthem for Doomed Youth' with one other poem from 'Conflict'. Write about:
- what the poems are about and what happens in them
- the poets' use of language
- the poets' use of form and structure
- the feelings and attitudes of the poets
- your response to the poems.

Refer closely to both poems. [20]

8 **OCR Anthology (*Towards a World Unknown*): Youth and Age**

Compare 'Holy Thursday' with one other poem from 'Youth and Age'. Write about:
- what the poems are about and what happens in them
- the poets' use of language
- the poets' use of form and structure
- the feelings and attitudes of the poets
- your response to the poems.

Refer closely to both poems. [20]

9 **WJEC Eduqas Anthology**

Compare 'Death of a Naturalist' with one other poem from the anthology. Write about:
- what the poems are about and what happens in them
- the poets' use of language
- the poets' use of form and structure
- the feelings and attitudes of the poets
- your response to the poems.

Refer closely to both poems. [20]

1 Read the poem below and answer the questions that follow.

The Song of the Old Mother

by W. B. Yeats

I rise in the dawn, and I kneel and blow

Till the seed of the fire flicker and glow;

And then I must scrub and bake and sweep

Till stars are beginning to blink and peep;

And the young lie long and dream in their bed

Of the matching ribbons for bosom and head,

And their day goes over in idleness,

And they sing if the wind but lift a tress:

While I must work because I am old,

And the seed of the fire gets feeble and cold.

a) Is the voice in the poem that of the poet or a persona? What sort of person is speaking?

_____

b) Where and when is it set? _____

c) Is there a strong, regular rhythm? If so, what effect does it have? _____

_____

d) Does it rhyme? If so, is there a regular rhyme scheme? What is the effect of the rhyme?

_____

e) What sort of imagery does the poet use? _____

f) Is there a story? If so, what is it? _____

g) What is the significance of the line 'And the seed of the fire gets feeble and cold'?

_____

h) What do you think the poem is really about? _____

i) What do you think is the poet's attitude / point of view? _____

_____

j) How does the poem make you feel? _____

_____ [20]

2 Read the two poems below and answer the question on a separate piece of paper.

Sonnet

by John Clare

I love to see the summer beaming forth

And white wool sack clouds sailing to the north

I love to see the wild flowers come again

And Mare drops stain with gold the meadow drain

And water lilies whiten on the floods

Where reed clumps rustle like a wind shook wood

Where from her hiding place the Moor Hen pushes

And seeks her flag nest floating in bull rushes

I like the willow leaning half way o'er

The clear deep lake to stand upon its shore

I love the hay grass when the flower head swings

To summer winds and insects happy wings

That sport about the meadow the bright day

And see bright beetles in the clear lake play.

The Eagle

by Alfred Tennyson

He clasps the crag with crooked hands;

Close to the sun in lonely lands,

Ring'd with the azure world he stands.

The wrinkled sea beneath him crawls;

He watches from his mountain walls,

And like a thunderbolt he falls.

Both 'Sonnet' and 'The Eagle' describe aspects of nature. What are the similarities and differences between the poets' feelings about the natural world and the ways in which they present those feelings? [20]

Mixed Exam-Style Questions

The following exam-style questions will help you to revise for:

- AQA Paper 1: Explorations in Creative Reading and Writing
- Edexcel Paper 1: Fiction and Imaginative Writing
- OCR Paper 2: Exploring Effects and Impact
- WJEC Eduqas Component 1: 20th Century Literature Reading and Creative Prose Writing

Depending on the exam board you are using, the style and format of the questions in these practice papers may be slightly different from what you will find in your actual exam paper. However, the knowledge and skills they require you to use apply equally to all the exam boards' papers.

Read the passage below and answer questions 1–6 that follow.

In this extract from 'Tickets, Please', D. H. Lawrence describes the trams of an English mining area, and the people who work on them, during the First World War.

To ride on these cars is always an adventure. Since we are in war-time, the drivers are men unfit for active service: cripples and hunchbacks. So they have the spirit of the devil in them. The ride becomes a steeple-chase.[1] Hurray! We have leapt in a clear jump over the canal bridges – now for the four-lane corner. With a shriek and a trail of sparks we are clear again. To be sure, a tram often leaps the rails – but what matter! It sits in a ditch till other trams come to haul it out. It is quite common for a car, packed with one solid mass of living people, to come to a dead halt in the midst of unbroken blackness, the heart of nowhere on a dark night, and for the driver and the girl conductor[2] to call, 'All get off – car's on fire!' Instead, however, of rushing out in a panic, the passengers stolidly reply: 'Get on – get on! We're not coming out. We're stopping where we are. Push on, George.' So till flames actually appear.

   The reason for this reluctance to dismount is that the nights are howlingly cold, black, and windswept, and a car is a haven of refuge. From village to village the miners travel, for a change of cinema, of girl, of pub. The trams are desperately packed. Who is going to risk himself in the black gulf outside, to wait perhaps an hour for another tram, then to see the forlorn notice 'Depot Only', because there is something wrong! Or to greet a unit of three bright cars all so tight with people that they sail past with a howl of derision. Trams that pass in the night.

   This, the most dangerous tram-service in England, as the authorities themselves declare, with pride, is entirely conducted by girls, and driven by rash young men, a little crippled, or by delicate young men, who creep forward in terror. The girls are fearless young hussies.[3] In their ugly blue uniform, skirts up to their knees, shapeless old peaked caps on their heads, they have all the *sang-froid*[4] of an old non-commissioned officer. With a tram packed with howling colliers, roaring hymns downstairs and a sort of antiphony[5] of obscenities upstairs, the lasses are perfectly at their ease. They pounce on the youths who try to evade their ticket-machine. They push off the men at the end of their distance. They are not going to be done in the eye – not they. They fear nobody – and everybody fears them.

   'Hello, Annie!'

   'Hello, Ted!'

   'Oh, mind my corn, Miss Stone. It's my belief you've got a heart of stone, for you've trod on it again.'

   'You should keep it in your pocket,' replies Miss Stone, and she goes sturdily upstairs in her high boots.

   'Tickets, please.'

---

[1] *steeple-chase* – a horse race over fences
[2] *conductor* – someone who sells tickets on a tram, bus or train
[3] *hussies* – cheeky or immoral girls
[4] *sang-froid* – coolness
[5] *antiphony* – singing in responses (usually in hymns)

1 Pick a phrase from the first paragraph that explains why the tram drivers are not fighting in the war.

_____ [1 mark]

2 Identify **two** dangerous things that often happen to the trams.

_____

_____ [2 marks]

3 According to the passage, which **one** of the following statements is **not** true?

a) Passengers are reluctant to leave the trams when told there's a fire.

b) The girls are easily shocked.

c) People are afraid of the girl conductors.

d) The kind of people who work on the trams has changed because of the war.

_____ [1 mark]

4 Look in detail at the first paragraph. How does the writer use language here to describe the atmosphere on the trams?

You could include the writer's choice of:
• words and phrases
• language features and techniques
• sentence forms.

Write your answer on a separate piece of paper. [8 marks]

5 Now think about the whole text.

This extract comes near the beginning of a short story.

How has the writer structured the text to interest you as a reader?

You could write about:
• what the writer focuses on at the beginning
• how and why he changes this focus
• any other structural features that interest you.

Write your answer on a separate piece of paper. [8 marks]

6 Think about the whole text.

What impression do you get of the people who work on the trams and who use them?

- Write about your own impressions of the people.
- Evaluate how the writer has created these impressions.
- Support your opinions with quotations from the text.

Write your answer on a separate piece of paper. [20 marks]

7 **Either**

Write a description suggested by this picture.

Or

Write a story that begins 'The minute I got off the train, I knew my life had changed for ever.'

[24 marks for content and organization and 16 marks for technical accuracy; total 40 marks]

The following exam-style questions will help you to revise for:

- AQA Paper 2: Writers' Viewpoints and Perspectives
- Edexcel Paper 2: Non-fiction and Transactional Writing
- OCR Paper 1: Communicating Information and Ideas
- WJEC Eduqas Component 2: 19th and 20th Century Non-fiction Reading and Transactional/Persuasive Writing

Read the sources below and answer questions 8–11 that follow.

Source A

In the extract below, taken from *Pictures from Italy*, Charles Dickens describes his visit to Florence in the 1840s.

But, how much beauty of another kind is here, when, on a fair clear morning, we look, from the summit of a hill, on Florence! See where it lies before us in a sun-lighted valley, bright with the winding Arno, and shut in by swelling hills; its domes, and towers, and palaces, rising from the rich country in a glittering heap, and shining in the sun like gold!

Magnificently stern and sombre are the streets of beautiful Florence; and the strong old piles of building make such heaps of shadow, on the ground and in the river, that there is another and a different city of rich forms and fancies, always lying at our feet. Prodigious palaces, constructed for defence, with small distrustful windows heavily barred, and walls of great thickness formed of huge masses of rough stone, frown, in their old sulky state, on every street. In the midst of the city – in the Piazza of the Grand Duke, adorned with beautiful statues and the Fountain of Neptune – rises the Palazzo Vecchio, with its enormous overhanging battlements, and the Great Tower that watches over the whole town. In its courtyard – worthy of the Castle of Otranto[1] in its ponderous gloom – is a massive staircase that the heaviest waggon and the stoutest team of horses might be driven up. Within it, is a Great Saloon, faded and tarnished in its stately decorations, and mouldering by grains, but recording yet, in pictures on its walls, the triumphs of the Medici and the wars of the old Florentine people. The prison is hard by, in an adjacent court-yard of the building – a foul and dismal place, where some men are shut up close, in small cells like ovens; and where others look through bars and beg; where some are playing draughts, and some are talking to their friends, who smoke, the while, to purify the air; and some are buying wine and fruit of women-vendors; and all are squalid, dirty, and vile to look at. 'They are merry enough, Signore,' says the jailer. 'They are all blood-stained here,' he adds, indicating, with his hand, three-fourths of the whole building. Before the hour is out, an old man, eighty years of age, quarrelling over a bargain with a young girl of seventeen, stabs her dead, in the market-place full of bright flowers; and is brought in prisoner, to swell the number.

[1] *Castle of Otranto* – the setting of a popular Gothic horror story of the same name

Source B

In this article for *The Times* (13 October 1982) Joyce Rackham discusses the problems caused by tourism in the Italian city of Florence.

FLORENCE: A city of dilemma

by Joyce Rackham

The bust of Benvenuto Cellini looks down sternly on the tourists littering the Ponte Vecchio. The younger ones loll – even sleep beneath him. Graffiti, although rarer than in the past, still scar some walls, and there is a very ugly souvenir stall. Yet the bridge is lined with fine shops, including jewellers whose best work follows Cellini's tradition of superb craftsmanship.

This scene reflects the dilemma of contemporary Florence – a matchless medieval city which has to stand up to the pressures, dirt and overcrowding of life in the 1980s.

Dr Silvio Abboni, a heart specialist who is also cultural assessor of the municipality, told me: 'We are victims of our big tourist boom. Florence was built as a fortress to withstand invaders. Now we must defend ourselves against too much mass tourism and potential speculators.'

Among his solutions are promoting itineraries off the beaten track, which will be published for visitors, as well as out of season attractions, both artistic and musical. He said that traffic jams could be intolerable in Florence and pointed to a new map showing plans to restrict car and bus parking and extend pedestrian precincts 'to allow city life to unfold in an orderly and pleasant manner'.

Dr Giorgio Chiarelli, Director of the Florence Tourist Board, said: 'We are a Renaissance city with about half a million inhabitants and an annual influx of around two million tourists.' He admitted that traffic pollution, litter and policing had been neglected, but said that this was changing.

Off-season tourism, with special art weekends from November to March, as well as extended shop and museum hours and more accommodation for young tourists, are intended to help ease pressures. The great Uffizi Gallery, the first public museum in the world, built by the Medici, celebrates its 400th anniversary this year. Professor Luciano Berti, its director since 1969, is also superintendent of the artistic and historic patrimony of Florence. 'Restoration is a continuous necessity and costs a great deal of money, and we don't have enough', he told me. 'We are most anxious that people see far more than the Uffizi. We cannot cope with a further growth of crowds. Since 1975 their volume has doubled.' He explained that dust from clothes and tramping feet, humidity from breath and wet clothes all have an adverse effect on paintings, many of which are now protected by glass. Crowd control measures are helping, as are the extended hours. Since August the Uffizi and most important museums, which used to close at 2pm, have been open until 7pm.

8 Read again the first five paragraphs of Source B (from 'The bust' to 'changing'). According to the article, which four of the following statements are TRUE?

- Shade the boxes of the ones you think are true.
- Choose a maximum of four statements.

a) The souvenir stall at the Ponte Vecchio is very attractive. ☐

b) There are shops on the bridge. ☐

c) There is no pollution in Florence. ☐

d) Dr Abboni believes the increase in tourists has been bad for Florence. ☐

e) Florence is a modern city. ☐

f) The jewellers produce some very good work. ☐

g) The authorities in Florence are encouraging tourists to go to less well-known parts of the city. ☐

h) Dr Abboni wants to ban tourists from Florence. ☐ [4 marks]

9 You need only to refer to Source A for this question.

How does Dickens use language to convey his impressions of Florence? Write your answer on a separate piece of paper. [12 marks]

10 You need to refer to Source A and Source B for this question.

Write a summary of the differences between the two descriptions of Florence. Use details from both sources. Write your answer on a separate piece of paper. [8 marks]

11 For this question you need to refer to the whole of Source A together with the whole of Source B.

Compare how the two writers convey their different reactions to the city of Florence.

In your answer you should:
*   compare their different reactions
*   compare the methods they use to convey their reactions
*   support your ideas with quotations from both texts. [16 marks]

Write your answer on a separate piece of paper.

12 a) 'Travel might broaden the mind, but tourism is destroying some of the world's most beautiful places. It is time we put the good of the planet before our own pleasure.'

Write an article for a broadsheet newspaper in which you explain your point of view on this statement. Write your answer on a separate piece of paper.

b) You have seen an advertisement in your local newspaper for a job as a travel guide. Write a letter applying for the job. Write your answer on a separate piece of paper.

[24 marks for content and organization; 16 marks for technical accuracy; total 40 marks]

Mixed Exam-Style Questions

The following exam-style questions will help you to revise for:
- AQA Paper 1
- Edexcel Paper 1
- OCR Paper 2
- WJEC Eduqas Component 1

Answer the question on the play you have studied.

13 *Julius Caesar* – Read the extract specified and answer the question below.

Here, Antony addresses the Roman people after the death of Caesar.

> **Act 3 Scene 2** *Read lines 74–85, from*
>
> ANTONY   Friends, Romans, countrymen, lend me your ears.
>
> *To*
>
> Come I to speak in Caesar's funeral.

Starting with this speech, explore how Shakespeare presents Antony as a politician. Write about:
- how Shakespeare presents Antony as a politician in this speech
- how Shakespeare presents Antony as a politician in the play as a whole.   [40 marks]

14 *Much Ado About Nothing* – Read the extract specified and answer the question below.

Here, Benedick approaches Beatrice after Hero has been rejected by Claudio.

> **Act 4 Scene 1** *Read lines 258–268, from*
>
> BENEDICK   Lady Beatrice, have you wept all this while?
>
> *To*
>
> BEATRICE   It is a man's office but not yours.

Starting with this conversation, write about how Shakespeare presents ideas about honour. Write about:
- how Shakespeare presents ideas about honour in this dialogue
- how Shakespeare presents ideas about honour in the play as a whole.   [40 marks]

15 *Macbeth* – Read the extract specified and answer the question below.

Here, Macbeth has murdered Duncan, and has returned with the blood-stained daggers.

> **Act 2 Scene 2** *Read lines 50–65, from*
>
> LADY MACBETH   Infirm of purpose!
>
> *To*
>
> LADY MACBETH   A little water clears us of this deed.

Explore how Shakespeare presents the relationship between Macbeth and Lady Macbeth. Refer to this extract and elsewhere in the play. **[40 marks]**

16 *Romeo and Juliet* – Read the extract specified and answer the question below.

Here, Romeo has just seen Juliet for the first time.

> **Act 1 Scene 5** *Read lines 42–51, from*
>
> ROMEO   O, she doth teach the torches to burn bright.
>
> *To*
>
> Did my heart love till now? Forswear it sight.
>
> For I ne'er saw true beauty till this night.

Starting with this speech, explore how Shakespeare presents Romeo's love for Juliet. Write about:
- how Shakespeare presents Romeo's feelings in this speech
- how Shakespeare presents Romeo's feelings in the play as a whole. **[40 marks]**

17 *The Tempest* – Read the extract specified and answer **both** questions below.

Here, Prospero has just discovered Miranda talking to Ferdinand and has cast a spell on him.

> **Act 1 Scene 2** *Read lines 477–486, from*
>
> MIRANDA   Beseech you, father!
>
> *To*
>
> MIRANDA   I have no ambition
>
> To see a godlier man.

a) How does Shakespeare present Prospero as a father in this extract? Refer closely to the extract in your answer.

b) Here Prospero is using magic to control Ferdinand and Miranda. Explain the importance of magic elsewhere in the play. **[40 marks]**

18 *The Merchant of Venice* – Read the extract specified and answer the question below.

Here, Portia, disguised as a man, pleads with Shylock to be merciful.

> **Act 4 Scene 1** *Read lines 181–194, from:*
>
> PORTIA   The quality of mercy is not strained.
>
> *To*
>
> It is an attribute of God Himself,
>
> And earthly power doth then show likest God's
>
> When mercy seasons justice.

Explore how Shakespeare presents ideas about justice and mercy. Refer to this extract and elsewhere in the play.   [40 marks]

19 *Twelfth Night* – Read the extract specified and answer **both** questions below.

Here, Viola, disguised as Cesario, has been sent by Orsino to court Olivia.

> **Act 1 Scene 5** *Read lines 253–265, from*
>
> VIOLA   If I did love you in my master's flame
>
> *To*
>   O, you should not rest
>
> Between the elements of air and earth
>
> But you should pity me.

a) How does Shakespeare present Viola's feelings in this extract? Refer closely to the extract in your answer.

b) Here Viola is in disguise. Explain the importance of disguise and mistaken identity elsewhere in the play.   [40 marks]

20 *Henry V* – Read the extract specified and answer **both** questions below.

Here, Henry passes sentence on the three traitors.

> **Act 2 Scene 2** *Read lines 162–178, from:*
>
> KING   God quit you in his mercy! Hear your sentence.
>
> *To*
>   Bear them hence.

a) Look at how Henry speaks and behaves here. What does this reveal to an audience about his character? Refer closely to the extract in your answer.

b) Write about how an audience might react to Henry's speeches at different points in the play.   [40 marks]

21 *Othello* – Read the extract specified and answer **both** questions below.

Here, Iago talks about his hatred of Othello and his plans.

> **Act 1 Scene 3** *Read lines 375–396, from*
>
> IAGO   Thus do I ever make my fool my purse:
>
> *To*
>
>   I have't. It is engendered. Hell and night
>
>   Must bring this monstrous birth to the world's light.

a) Look at how Iago speaks and behaves here. What does this reveal to an audience about his character and motivation? Refer closely to the extract in your answer.

b) Write about how an audience might react to Iago at different points in the play.   [40 marks]

Mixed Exam-Style Questions

The following exam-style questions will help you to revise for:

- AQA Paper 1
- Edexcel Paper 2
- OCR Paper 1
- WJEC Eduqas Component 2

Answer the question on the novel you have studied.

22 **Mary Shelley: *Frankenstein*** (Answer **both** parts of the question.)

In this extract, Victor Frankenstein has been confronted by the creature in the mountains.

> **Read Chapter 10**
>
> *From*
>
> 'Abhorred monster! Fiend that thou art! The tortures of hell are too mild a vengence for thy crimes. Wretched devil! You reproach me with your creation; come on, then, that I may extinguish the spark which I so negligently bestowed.'
>
> *To*
>
> 'Begone! I will not hear you. There can be no community between you and me; we are enemies. Begone, or let us try our strength in a fight, in which one must fall.'

Starting with this extract, explore to what extent and how Shelley makes the monster sympathetic.

a) Write about whether and how Shelley presents the monster sympathetically in this extract.

b) Explain how Shelley presents the monster elsewhere in the novel.   [40 marks]

23 **Sir Arthur Conan Doyle: *The Sign of Four*** (Answer **both** parts of the question.)

In this extract, Miss Morstan has come to Sherlock Holmes for help.

> **Read Chapter 2**
>
> *From*
>
> Miss Morstan entered the room with a firm step and an outward composure of manner.
>
> *To*
>
> I relapsed into my chair.

Starting with this extract, write about how Conan Doyle presents Miss Morstan and about her role in the novel. Write about:

- how he presents Miss Morstan in this extract
- how he presents Miss Morstan in the novel as a whole.   [40 marks]

24 **Charlotte Brontë: *Jane Eyre***

In this extract, Jane has been locked in the Red Room by her aunt.

> **Read Chapter 2**
>
> *From*
>
> 'Unjust! – unjust!' said my reason, forced by the agonising stimulus into precocious though transitory power: and Resolve, equally wrought up, instigated some strange expedient to achieve escape from insupportable oppression – as running away, or, if that could not be effected, never eating or drinking more, and letting myself die.
>
> *To*
>
> It must have been most irksome to find herself bound by a hard-wrung pledge to stand in the stead of a parent to a strange child she could not love, and to see an uncongenial alien permanently intruded on her own family group.

Explore how Brontë presents Jane as an outsider in this extract and elsewhere in the novel. [40 marks]

25 **Jane Austen: *Pride and Prejudice*** (Answer **both** parts of the question.)

In this extract, Austen describes Elizabeth's visit to Pemberley.

> **Read Chapter 43 (Volume 3, Chapter 1)**
>
> *From*
>
> The housekeeper came; a respectable-looking, elderly woman, much less fine, and more civil, than she had any notion of finding her.
>
> *To*
>
> 'Perhaps we might be deceived.'
>
> 'That is not very likely; our authority was too good.'

Starting with this extract, explore how Austen describes Elizabeth's changing feelings towards Darcy. Write about:
- how she writes about Elizabeth's feelings in this extract
- how she writes about Elizabeth's changing feelings in the novel as a whole. [40 marks]

26 **Charles Dickens: *Great Expectations*** (Answer **both** parts of the question.)

In this extract, Pip is visiting Miss Havisham for the first time. She has asked him to call for Estella.

> **Read Chapter 8**
>
> *From*
>
> 'Call Estella,' she repeated, flashing a look at me. 'You can do that. Call Estella. At the door.'
>
> *To*
>
> 'I am not sure that I shouldn't like to see her again, but I should like to go home now.'
>
> 'You shall go soon,' said Miss Havisham, aloud. 'Play the game out.'

a) Explore how Dickens portrays Pip's relationship with Estella in this extract.

b) In this extract Pip meets two female characters who will be important in his life. Explain how Dickens portrays relationships between men and women elsewhere in the novel. [40 marks]

27 **Robert Louis Stevenson:** *The Strange Case of Dr Jekyll and Mr Hyde*

In this extract, Stevenson describes one of Mr Utterson's Sunday walks with his cousin, Mr Enfield.

> **Read Chapter 1 ('The Story of the Door')**
>
> *From*
>
> No doubt the feat was easy to Mr Utterson; for he was undemonstrative at the best, and even his friendship seemed to be founded in a similar catholicity of good-nature.
>
> *To*
>
> 'Indeed?' said Mr Utterson, with a slight change of voice, 'and what was that?'

Write about how Stevenson uses Utterson to explore 'the strange case'. In your response:
- refer to the extract and the novel as a whole
- show your understanding of the characters and events in the novel
- refer to the contexts of the novel.   [40 marks]

28 **Charles Dickens:** *A Christmas Carol* (Answer **both** parts of the question.)

In this extract, the Ghost of Christmas Present has taken Scrooge to observe the Cratchits' Christmas.

> **Read Stave (Chapter) 3 ('The Second of the Three Spirits')**
>
> *From*
>
> 'And how did little Tim behave?' asked Mrs Cratchit, when she had rallied Bob on his credulity and Bob had hugged his daughter to his heart's content.
>
> *To*
>
> 'I see a vacant seat,' replied the Ghost, 'in the poor chimney-corner, and a crutch without an owner, carefully preserved. If these shadows remain unaltered by the Future, the child will die.'

Starting with this extract, explore how Dickens writes about the 'spirit of Christmas':
- how he writes about the spirit of Christmas in this extract
- how he writes about the spirit of Christmas in the novel as a whole.   [40 marks]

29 **H. G. Wells:** *The War of the Worlds*

In this extract, the artilleryman explains to the narrator what he thinks will happen to human beings in the future.

> **Read Book 2 Chapter 7**
>
> *From*
>
> 'Eh!' he said, with his eyes shining. 'I've thought it out, eh?'
>
> *To*
>
> 'What's the good of going on with such lies?' said the artilleryman. 'There's men who'd do it cheerful. What nonsense to pretend there isn't!'
>
> And I succumbed to his conviction.

Explore how Wells uses the Martian invasion to make readers think about how humans might react to oppressive power. [40 marks]

30 **George Eliot:** *Silas Marner*

In this extract, Eliot describes how the congregation at Lantern Yard find Silas guilty of a crime he did not commit, and how he loses his faith as a result.

> **Read Chapter 1**
>
> *From*
>
> Silas was still looking at his friend.
>
> *To*
>
> In little more than a month from that time, Sarah was married to William Dane; and not long afterwards it was known to the brethren in Lantern Yard that Silas Marner had departed from the town.

Write about how Eliot portrays faith and religion. In your response:
*   refer to the extract and the novel as a whole
*   show your understanding of the characters and events in the novel
*   refer to the contexts of the novel. [40 marks]

Mixed Exam-Style Questions

The following exam-style questions will help you to revise for:
- AQA Paper 2
- Edexcel Paper 1
- OCR Paper 1
- WJEC Eduqas Component 2

Answer the question on the text you have studied.

31 **J. B. Priestley: *An Inspector Calls***

How does Priestley present the character of Mr Birling in *An Inspector Calls*?
Refer to the context of the play in your answer.   [40 marks]

32 **Willy Russell: *Blood Brothers***

> **Read the narrator's song near the end of Act 1.**

Use this extract and your knowledge of the whole play to answer the question.
How does Russell use the narrator in *Blood Brothers*?   [40 marks]

33 **Alan Bennett: *The History Boys***

How does Bennett present Irwin as a teacher in *The History Boys*? Write about:
- what Irwin does and says
- how Bennett presents Irwin in the play.   [40 marks]

34 **Dennis Kelly: *DNA***

> **Read Leah's speech in Act 1 (pages 26–27).**

Answer **both** parts of the question.

a) How does Kelly present ideas about friendship in this speech?

b) Write about another moment in the play when ideas about friendship are explored.   [40 marks]

35 **Simon Stephens: *The Curious Incident of the Dog in the Night-Time***

> **Read Part One (pages 13–14) – dialogue between Siobhan and Christopher.**

Use this extract and your knowledge of the whole play to answer the question.
How does Stephens present the character of Siobhan in *The Curious Incident of the Dog in the Night-Time*?   [40 marks]

36 **Shelagh Delaney: *A Taste of Honey***

How does Delaney present attitudes to sex in *A Taste of Honey*? Write about:
- the different attitudes presented in the play
- how Delaney presents these attitudes.   [40 marks]

37 **Harold Brighouse: *Hobson's Choice***

How does Brighouse explore the role of women in society?
You must refer to the context of the play in your answer. [40 marks]

38 **R. C. Sherriff: *Journey's End***

In Act 1, Osborne and Stanhope discuss 'hero-worship'.

What does Sherriff mean by 'hero-worship' and what is its significance in the play?
You must refer to the context of the play in your answer. [40 marks]

39 **Charlotte Keatley: *My Mother Said I Never Should***

Read Act 1 Scene 4 and answer **both** parts of the question.

a) How does Keatley explore women's attitudes to men in this scene?

b) Write about how she explores women's attitudes to men in another part of the play. [40 marks]

40 **William Golding: *Lord of the Flies***

How does Golding use symbols in *Lord of the Flies*?
You must refer to the context of the novel in your answer. [40 marks]

41 **AQA Anthology: *Telling Tales***

How do writers explore relationships between men and women in 'Chemistry' and one other story from *Telling Tales*?
Write about:
* relationships between men and women in the two stories
* how the writers present relationships between men and women. [40 marks]

42 **George Orwell: *Animal Farm***

> **Read the first two pages of Chapter 2 (the death of Major).**

Answer **both** parts of the question.

a) How does Orwell present the pigs in this extract?

b) Explore another part of the novel where the pigs change. [40 marks]

43 **Kazuo Ishiguro: *Never Let Me Go***

How does Ishiguro present the character of Tommy in *Never Let Me Go*? Write about:
* what Tommy does and says
* how others react to Tommy. [40 marks]

44 **Meera Syal: *Anita and Me***

> Read Chapter 1 pages 22–23.

Answer **both** parts of the question.

a) How does Syal present Meena's relationship with her parents in this part of the novel?

b) Explore another part of the novel where Syal writes about Meena's relationship with her parents. [40 marks]

45 **Stephen Kelman: *Pigeon English***

How does Kelman present gang culture in *Pigeon English*? Write about:
- how gangs and gang members behave in *Pigeon English*
- how Kelman presents gangs and gang members. [40 marks]

46 **Susan Hill: *The Woman in Black***

> Read the first two pages of the second chapter ('A London Particular').

Use this part of the novel and your knowledge of the whole novel to answer the question.
How does Hill use the character of Arthur Kipps in *The Woman in Black* to affect the reader's response to the story? [40 marks]

47 **Jeanette Winterson: *Oranges Are Not the Only Fruit***

> Read 'Exodus' pages 21–22 (up to 'And it was.')

Use this part of the novel and your knowledge of the whole novel to answer the question.
How does Winterson present the relationship between Jeanette and her mother in *Oranges Are Not the Only Fruit*? [40 marks]

The following exam-style questions will help you to revise for:

- AQA Paper 2
- Edexcel Paper 2
- OCR Paper 2
- WJEC Eduqas Component 1

AQA Anthology

Either

48 Compare the way poets present danger in 'The Charge of the Light Brigade' and one other poem from 'Power and Conflict'. [20 marks]

Or

49 Compare the way poets present parting in 'When We Two Parted' and one other poem from 'Love and Relationships'. [20 marks]

Edexcel Anthology

Either

50 Read 'Nettles'. Choose one other poem from 'Time and Place'. Compare how the poets' feelings are presented in the two poems. [20 marks]

Or

51 Read 'Poppies'. Choose one other poem from 'Conflict'. Compare how the poets present the effects of war in both poems. [20 marks]

Or

52 Read 'Where the Picnic Was'. Choose one other poem from 'Time and Place'. Compare how the poets write about memories in both poems. [20 marks]

WJEC Eduqas Anthology

53 Answer both part (a) and part (b).

a) Read 'Hawk Roosting' by Ted Hughes.
   Write about the way Hughes presents power in this poem.

b) Now read 'Ozymandias' by Percy Bysshe Shelley.
   Write about the ways Shelley presents power in this poem and compare these with the ways Hughes presents power in 'Hawk Roosting'. [20 marks]

Mixed Exam-Style Questions

OCR Anthology

Either

54 **Love and Relationships**

Read 'An Arundel Tomb' and 'The Soldier' (opposite) and then answer **both** parts of the question.

a) Compare how the poets express feelings about death and memory. [20 marks]

b) Explore in detail how one other poem from the anthology presents memories. [20 marks]

Or

55 **Conflict**

Read 'The Man He Killed' and 'The Soldier' (both opposite) and then answer **both** parts of the question.

a) Compare how the poems present feelings about war. [20 marks]

b) Explore in detail one other poem from the anthology which presents feelings about war and its effects. [20 marks]

Or

56 **Youth and Age**

Read 'Out, Out' and 'The Soldier' (on the page opposite) and then answer **both** parts of the question.

a) Compare how the poets write about the death of a young person. [20 marks]

b) Explore in detail one other poem from the anthology that presents death or injury to a young person. [20 marks]

The following exam-style question will help you to revise for:

- AQA Paper 2
- Edexcel Paper 2
- WJEC Eduqas Component 2

57 Read the two poems below and answer both questions.

The Man He Killed

by Thomas Hardy

'Had he and I but met
By some old ancient inn
We should have sat us down to wet
Right many a nipperkin!

'But ranged as infantry
And staring face to face,
I shot at him as he at me,
And killed him in his place.

'I shot him dead because –
Because he was my foe,
Just so: my foe of course he was;
That's clear enough; although

'He thought he'd 'list, perhaps,
Off-hand like – just as I –
Was out of work – had sold his traps –
No other reason why.

'Yes; quaint and curious war is!
You shoot a fellow down
You'd treat if met where any bar is,
Or help to half-a-crown.'

The Soldier

by Rupert Brooke

If I should die, think only this of me:
That there's some corner of a foreign field
That is for ever England. There shall be
In that rich earth a richer dust concealed;
A dust whom England bore, shaped, made aware,
Gave, once, her flowers to love, her ways to roam,
A body of England's, breathing English air,
Washed by the rivers, blest by suns of home.

And think, this heart, all evil shed away,
A pulse the eternal mind, no less
Gives somewhere back the thoughts by England
   given;
Her sights and sounds; dreams happy as her day;
And laughter, learnt of friends; and gentleness,
In hearts at peace, under an English heaven.

a) How does Hardy present the speaker's feelings about being a soldier in 'The Man He Killed'?

b) Both 'The Man He Killed' and 'The Soldier' are about going to war. What are the similarities and differences between the ways in which the poets present feelings about war?

[20 marks]

Answers

GCSE Grades

Please note that we cannot give equivalents between numerical marks and GCSE grades, as these are determined by the exam board after the examination has been taken.

Pages 4–5 Key Concepts from Key Stage 3

1. a) Beth [1]; she is described as speaking 'contentedly'. The other girls 'grumbled', 'sighed' or sniffed. [2]
2. He is away in the army. [1]
3. a) That he might get killed. [1]
    b) They might not want to upset each other (or any reasonable answer). [1]
4. a) Giving up small things for a reason. [1]
    b) Someone who likes reading. [1]
5. They have very little money and even if they gave it to the government it would not make a lot of difference. [2]
6. Beth is saying what she wanted to spend her money on before they were told there were to be no presents, [1] implying she is not now going to spend it. [1] Amy tells us what she is planning to spend her money on. [1]
7. Suggested content:
*   They are poor / do not have much money, and so will not get any Christmas presents.
*   There are four sisters. They live with their mother, and their father is away. As he is 'where the fighting is' he seems to be in the army, fighting in a war.
*   They seem to be a close, quite happy family, as Beth says they have 'Father and Mother, and each other', to which they all respond positively.
*   They all seem to have the same love and respect for their parents and are all worried about their father, which makes them sad.
*   The girls are honest about their feelings. Although they understand why they are asked to make 'sacrifices', they still want things for themselves.
*   They have different interests: Jo likes reading, Beth music and Amy drawing. Meg just seems to like 'pretty things'.
*   It is Meg who expresses their problem, reporting Mother's reasoning, but it is Jo who argues logically that they should still buy presents. This suggests that she has a mind of her own and is intelligent.
*   Beth is the most placid and accepting of the girls, as well as the least assertive. Amy might be seen as selfish as she is so quick to take up Jo's idea and says she 'shall' get the pencils, but she could just be more decisive.
    [5 marks – 1 for one or two of these or similar points, 3 for about half of them, 5 for most of them and perhaps some original points]
8. Possible ideas for your letter:
*   Thank your grandfather for the money. Describe what you have spent it on / what you will spend it on. Explain why you decided to buy it. Say what your family/friends think about it. Mention that it will remind you of him. Tell him what you have been doing in school / after school / during the holidays. Say something about your family. Mention things that he might remember. Ask about his life and send your best wishes to other family members.
    An excellent answer (17–20 marks) will:
*   Show a full awareness of purpose (thanks), audience (grandfather) and form (informal letter).
*   Engage the reader's interest throughout, perhaps using humour and/or emotive language.

*   Include a full range of techniques, such as correct use of first and second person, modal verbs, conditionals, questions.
*   Present a variety of ideas, using a sophisticated range of vocabulary and sentence structure.
*   Use paragraphs and connectives effectively.
*   Achieve a high level of accuracy in punctuation and grammar.
*   Achieve a high level of accuracy in spelling.

Pages 6–15 Revise Questions

Page 7 Quick Test
1. No, where. 2. It's. 3. Whether, to.
4. Practice.

Page 9 Quick Test
1. 'Where's my hamster?' Leo cried.
2. He had gone. There was no doubt about it.
3. Maureen, who lived next door, searched her bins.
4. Maureen's son, however, found Hammy in the kitchen.

Page 11 Quick Test
1. d 2. a 3. b 4. c

Page 13 Quick Test
1. First – to give order.
2. On the other hand – to introduce a contrasting idea or point of view.
3. Before – to express passing time.
4. Therefore – to express cause and effect.

Page 15 Quick Test
1. Jay and I were put on detention.
2. I saw you on Saturday.
3. You were the best player we had.
4. After we had sung the first number, we did a dance.

Pages 16–17 Practice Questions

1. were, weather, pouring, excited, wait, metres, There, which, coming, definitely.
    [1 mark for each correct spelling – maximum 10]
2. a) Peter Kowalski, who was the tallest boy in the class, easily won the high jump.
    b) 'What are you doing in the sand pit?' shouted Miss O'Connor. 'Get out of there at once!'
    c) Francesca won medals for the long jump, the high jump and the relay.
    d) I wasn't entered in any of the races because I'm hopeless at running.
    e) Jonathan finished last. However, he was pleased with his time.
    [1 mark for each – maximum 5]
3. a) (i) Julia stayed off school because she had a stomach ache.
        (ii) He might be in the changing rooms or he might have already left.
    b) (i) Michael, who has a really loud voice, announced the results.
        (ii) The form with the best results won a cup, which was presented by Mr Cadogan.
    c) (i) Maria, who had won the discus competition, went home early because she was feeling sick.
    [1 mark for each – maximum 5]
4. a) Hayley and I are going to town tomorrow.
    b) You can come with us if you want to.
    c) We were very pleased with what we bought.
    d) I do not (don't) know anything about what they did at school.
    e) I am not truanting again because I want to get my GCSEs.
    [1 mark for each – maximum 5]

5. (1) As well as (2) As a result of (3) also (4) Consequently (5) However [5]
6. experience [1] was [1] visited [1] stories [1], stars' [1] biographies [1]. Therefore, [1], she and I [1] Bingley Park [1]. The [1] [Maximum 10]

Pages 18–31 Revise Questions

Page 19 Quick Test
1. Openly stated. 2. Yes. 3. Yes.
4. No.

Page 21 Quick Test
1. The writer. 2. The reader. 3. No.

Page 23 Quick Test
1. Yes. 2. Yes. 3. No.

Page 25 Quick Test
1. Quotation and paraphrase.
2. Everything that is in the original text.
3. When it does not fit easily into the sentence.
4. Point Evidence Explanation (or exploration).

Page 27 Quick Test
1. Horse and oats. 2. Was munching.
3. Old. 4. On. 5. Thoughtfully.

Page 29 Quick Test
1. Personification. 2. Alliteration.
3. Simile. 4. Metaphor.

Page 31 Quick Test
1. b, c, d, a 2. a, d, c, b 3. c, a, b, d

Pages 32–33 Review Questions

1. a) except, accept b) effect, affect
    c) allowed, aloud d) right, write
    e) whose, who's
    [1 mark for each pair – maximum 5]
2. 'Don't you think we should wait for him?' asked Eve.
    'Not at all,' Henry replied. 'He never waits for us.'
    'Well, that's true,' Eve replied, 'but he doesn't know the way.'
    [½ mark for each correct punctuation mark – maximum 10]
3. This is a suggested answer only. There are other ways of doing it.
    Henry and Eve waited for another ten minutes but Joel did not arrive, so they left without him and walked to the bus stop. There was no-one there, suggesting they had just missed the bus. Henry was very annoyed with Joel. However, Eve told him to calm down and forget about Joel. After an uneventful journey, they got off the bus by the lake, which looked eerie in the moonlight. Having sat down on a grassy bank, they took their sandwiches and drinks out of the bag. Henry felt a hand on his shoulder.
    [Maximum 10 marks]
4. b, d, f, h, i [Maximum 5 marks]
5. a) pizzas b) latches
    c) mosquitoes d) sheep
    e) donkeys f) stadia
    g) qualities h) churches
    i) women j) hypotheses
    [½ mark for each – maximum 5]
6. e, c, a, d, b [Maximum 5 marks]

Pages 34–35 Practice Questions

1.
*   Nobody greeted him cheerfully.
*   People did not ask him to come and see them.
*   Beggars did not beg from him.
*   Children did not ask him for the time.
*   Nobody asked him the way anywhere.
    [Maximum 4 marks]

2.

Marks	Skills	Examples of possible content
7–8	• You have analysed the effects of the choice of language. • You have used an appropriate range of quotations. • You have used sophisticated subject terminology appropriately.	The first complex sentence seems quite light-hearted, the direct speech reflecting a polite greeting, such as people might make in the street, but the sentence starts with 'Nobody', so we know Scrooge is not like others. The next sentence builds a list of those who avoid Scrooge, starting each clause with 'no' before giving an innocuous phrase such as 'what it was o'clock'. The last sentence gives us a sense of evil, 'even the blindmen's dogs' implying that a dislike of Scrooge is natural and instinctive.
5–6	• You have clearly explained the effects of the choice of language. • You have used a range of relevant quotations. • You have used subject terminology appropriately.	In three sentences, each one longer than the last, the writer gives lists of different sorts of people, starting phrases with the repeated 'no', to give a general negative impression. When he imagines what the dogs might say he uses the adjectives 'dark' and 'evil' to show that Scrooge is feared.

[Maximum 8 marks]

3. a) 'With you and your sister I could gang anywhere'; 'the pleasure of your company'. [Maximum 2 marks]
    b) They show that Lamb enjoys being with Wordsworth / that they are good friends. [Maximum 2 marks]
4. b, c, e [Maximum 3 marks]
5.

Marks	Skills	Examples of possible content
7–8	• You have given a perceptive interpretation of both texts. • You have synthesized evidence from the texts. • You have used appropriate quotations from both texts.	Although the writers have opposite views – Weston is a 'city-hater' but Lamb never wants to 'see a mountain in my life' – they are both careful not to insult people who have the opposite view ('I could gang anywhere'; 'Sorry, Londoners'). Lamb lists things like 'crowded streets' that he likes. These are the things Weston hates, calling it 'dirty' and 'noisy'. Weston knows 'it's meant to be…exciting' and this is clearly Lamb's view.
5–6	• You have started to interpret both texts. • You have shown clear connections between texts. • You have used relevant quotations from both texts.	Lamb explains that he has always lived in London so cannot see the attraction of the countryside. Weston, on the other hand, calls the country 'home' and thinks this is why he is bored with the city. Lamb loves the shops, the theatre and even the 'wickedness', but Weston can only see how 'expensive' it is and how everyone is 'bad-tempered'.

[Maximum 8 marks]

Pages 36–51 Revise Questions

Page 37 Quick Test
1. The beginning.   2. First.
3. The inciting incident.
4. One who knows everything.
Page 39 Quick Test
1. Simile.
2. Personification / pathetic fallacy.
3. Metaphor.   4. Literal imagery.
Page 41 Quick Test
1. The main character.

2. A character who opposes the protagonist.
3. Something that happens to get the story going.
4. An event that changes the direction of the story.
Page 43 Quick Test
1. George lived alone.
2. Like ancient gravestones.
3. Love loyalty / apparent affection.
4. His teeth were rarely seen.
Page 45 Quick Test
1. Biography.   2. Letter.   3. Diary.

4. Autobiography.
Page 47 Quick Test
2 (news report).
Page 49 Quick Test
1. To argue your point of view.
2. The governors.   3. Letter.
Page 51 Quick Test
1. Yours sincerely.
2. Yours faithfully.
3. Yours faithfully.
4. Yours sincerely.

Pages 52–53 Review Questions

1. Currer Bell. [1]
2. b [1]
3. They were not obviously male or female / they could be either. [1]
4. They were worried that publishers would be prejudiced against female writers. [1]
5. They gave her some good advice and she acted on it, leading to publication. [1]
6. Look at the mark scheme below, decide which description is closest to your answer and then decide which mark to give yourself. See 'Skills' column of table above (for pages 34–35 Practice Questions, Q5).

Marks	Examples of possible content
7–8	It took Brontë a long time to get published. She had to work out the 'puzzle' of why no-one was interested and look for advice. Fordyce, on the other hand, was published quickly and is often asked for advice by other poets. They also had very different experiences of being a woman poet. Brontë had a 'vague impression' that her sex would be a disadvantage, but Fordyce, who was 'welcomed with enthusiasm' by other poets, feels it was a positive thing for her.
5–6	The Brontës thought they might be 'looked on with prejudice' because they were women, whereas Fordyce thinks her gender was an advantage ('we don't get enough women'). Fordyce wrote to magazines and performed her poetry live, but for Brontë the only way was to write to publishers, who did not reply.

[Maximum 8 marks]

7. Look at the mark scheme below, decide which description is closest to your answer and then decide which mark to give yourself. See 'Skills' column of table above (for pages 34–35 Practice Questions, Q2).

Marks	Examples of possible content
10–12	Fordyce gives advice in a clear, colloquial tone, as if she is talking to a friend: 'All I can do is say'. She is also modest, using the noun 'luck' three times and the adjective 'lucky' once, though this is balanced by the repetition of references to 'hard work'. She uses short, often simple sentences – 'It wasn't that hard for me' – which helps make the process seem simple. Using the metaphor 'magic key' in the first paragraph could make readers think she is saying she can't help, but this impression is contradicted by the rest of the passage, as she does try to help.
7–9	Fordyce writes in a chatty, straightforward way, getting straight to the point with 'People often ask me'. She uses a metaphor, 'magic key', to show that there is no easy answer, but her tone is helpful. She emphasizes that this is her personal experience by constant use of the first person.

[Maximum 12 marks]

1. Look at the mark scheme below, decide which description is closest to your answer and then decide which mark to give yourself.

Marks	Skills	Examples of possible content
10–12	• You have analysed the effects of the choice of language and structure. • You have used an appropriate range of quotations. • You have used sophisticated subject terminology appropriately.	The writer's tone is quite serious and authoritative. He begins with a controversial assertion and develops an argument to back it up. The expression 'confounds the moralist' suggests that he is dealing with a moral problem. He uses hyperbole to show he loves dogs ('the great soul'). Other rhetorical devices he uses include the rhetorical question ('Where will the process end?') and the list of three, combined with alliteration ('crib, cabin, and confine'). He uses emotive language to make us feel sorry for the small dogs: 'frets the puny body to decay'.
7–9	• You have clearly explained the effects of the choice of language and structure. • You have used a range of relevant quotations. • You have used subject terminology appropriately.	The writer uses Standard English and sounds as if he knows what he's talking about. He uses impressive phrases like the 'great soul' to show he loves dogs and feels sad that they are made into 'puny' animals. He uses long, complex sentences to explain his ideas. He uses a rhetorical question ('Where will the process end?') to make us think about the consequences of breeding these dogs.

[Maximum 12 marks]

2.

Marks	Skills	Examples of possible content
15–18	• You have compared ideas and perspectives in a perceptive way. • You have analysed methods used to convey ideas and perspectives. • You have used a range of appropriate quotations.	Both these writers are very passionate about their subject. The first writer attacks those who breed small dogs by making the dogs sound like victims ('all eyes and nerves') but also calls them 'pampered'. Hanlon picks up on this but cannot see what's wrong with pampering – she sees it as a sign of love. Her tone is chatty and personal, while his is impersonal and authoritative.
10–14	• You have compared ideas and perspectives in a clear and relevant way. • You have explained clearly methods used to convey ideas and perspectives. • You have used relevant quotations from both texts.	The writer in *The Times* uses rhetorical devices to convince his readers. He claims to love dogs but is against breeding small dogs and treating them like toys. Hanlon defends people who have small dogs, saying those who attack them are just having a go at celebrities. She too uses rhetorical questions.

[Maximum 18 marks]

3. This task is marked for content and organization, and for technical accuracy.

Content and Organization		
22–24	**Content:**	• You have communicated convincingly and compellingly throughout. • Your tone, style and register assuredly match purpose, form and audience. • You have used an extensive and ambitious vocabulary with sustained crafting of linguistic devices.
	Organization:	• Your writing is highly structured and developed, including a range of integrated and complex ideas. • Your paragraphs are fluently linked with integrated discourse markers. • You have used a variety of structural features in an inventive way.
19–21	**Content:**	• You have communicated convincingly. • Your tone, style and register consistently match purpose, form and audience. • You have used an extensive vocabulary with evidence of conscious crafting of linguistic devices.
	Organization:	• Your writing is structured and developed, including a range of engaging and complex ideas. • You have used paragraphs consistently with integrated discourse markers. • You have used a variety of structural features effectively.
16–18	**Content:**	• You have communicated clearly and effectively. • Your tone, style and register match purpose, form and audience. • You have used an increasingly sophisticated vocabulary with a range of appropriate linguistic devices.
	Organization:	• Your writing is engaging, including a range of engaging and detailed connected ideas. • You have used paragraphs coherently, with integrated discourse markers. • You have used structural features effectively.
13–15	**Content:**	• You have communicated clearly. • Your tone, style and register generally match purpose, form and audience. • You have used vocabulary for effect with a range of linguistic devices.
	Organization:	• Your writing is engaging, including a range of connected ideas. • You have usually used paragraphs coherently, with a range of discourse markers. • You have usually used structural features effectively.

Technical Accuracy	
13–16	• You have consistently demarcated sentences accurately. • You have used a wide range of punctuation with a high level of accuracy. • You have used a full range of sentence forms for effect. • You have used Standard English consistently and accurately, with secure control of grammatical structures. • You have achieved a high level of accuracy in spelling, including ambitious vocabulary. • Your use of vocabulary is extensive and ambitious.
9–12	• You have usually demarcated sentences accurately. • You have used a range of punctuation, usually accurately. • You have used a variety of sentence forms for effect. • You have used Standard English appropriately, with control of grammatical structures. • You have spelled most words, including complex and irregular words, correctly. • Your use of vocabulary is increasingly sophisticated.

Page 57 Quick Test
1. False.   2. False.   3. False.   4. True.
Page 59 Quick Test
1. Soliloquy.   2. Dialogue.
3. Plot.   4. Theme

Page 61 Quick Test
1. False.   2. False.   3. True.   4. True.
Page 63 Quick Test
1. Metaphor / rhetorical question.
2. Oxymoron.   3. Rhetorical
question.   4. Rhyming couplet.

1. Look at the mark scheme below, decide which description is closest to your answer and then decide which mark to give yourself.

Marks	Skills	Examples of possible content
7–8	• You have analysed the use of structural features. • You have chosen an appropriate range of examples. • You have used a range of subject terminology accurately.	The writer wants to create an air of mystery and to keep the reader curious. He distances the death of Sir Charles by describing it in Dr Mortimer's speech. In his first paragraph he talks about Sir Charles's health, which the reader might think explains his death, but he ends with the word 'catastrophe'. This makes us want to know what the awful thing was. The next paragraph is about his experience on the night of the death and builds up to his revelation that there was more to it than was revealed at the inquest. This adds to the mystery but he still does not reveal his information. Holmes asks him questions that might be in the reader's mind, while delaying the shock revelation.
5–6	• You have clearly explained the effect of structural features. • You have chosen relevant examples. • You have used subject terminology accurately.	The doctor builds up to a revelation by describing following Sir Charles's footprints. At the end he mentions that he knows something no-one else has noticed but keeps back the information until Holmes questions him. This makes the fact that 'they were the footprints of a gigantic hound' have more impact on the reader.

[Maximum 8 marks]

2.

Marks	Skills	Examples of possible content
16–20	• You have critically evaluated the text in a detailed way. • You have analysed a range of the writer's methods. • You have used a range of relevant quotations to support your views.	We are not told anything about the doctor's character, but the fact that he is a professional, scientific man implies he is a reliable witness. This is confirmed by his suspicion that Sir Charles's illness was 'chimerical', suggesting he is not easily convinced of things. He describes how he 'checked and corroborated' the evidence from the inquest, implying that he is both thorough and independent-minded. The fact that he has done this, and the careful and detailed description he gives, make the reader more inclined to accept his story than if it had been told in a sensational way.
11–15	• You have clearly evaluated the text. • You have clearly explained the effect of the writer's methods. • You have used some relevant quotations to support your views.	The story of finding the footprints is far-fetched but the use of Dr Mortimer to tell it makes it more believable. This is because he is a doctor and he tells the story in a calm way, remembering details: 'I noted that there were no other footsteps save those of Barrymore on the soft gravel.' When the writer says 'his voice sank almost to a whisper', the reader gets the impression that he is scared and shocked.

[Maximum 20 marks]

3. Look at the mark scheme on Page 130 (for pages 54–55 Practice Questions, Q3). This task is marked for content and organization, and for technical accuracy.

For all questions, look at the mark scheme below.

Marks	Skills
18–20	• You have responded to the task in an exploratory and critical way. • You have used precise, appropriate references to support your interpretation. • You have analysed the writer's methods using subject terminology appropriately. • You have explored the effects of the writer's methods. • You have explored links between text and ideas/context.
15–17	• You have responded to the task in a thoughtful, developed way. • You have used appropriate references to support your interpretation. • You have examined the writer's methods using subject terminology effectively. • You have examined the effects of the writer's methods. • You have thoughtfully considered links between text and ideas/context.
11–14	• You have responded to the task in a clear way. • You have used references effectively to support your explanation. • You have clearly explained the writer's methods using relevant subject terminology. • You have understood the effects of the writer's methods. • You have clearly understood links between text and ideas/context.

[Maximum 20 marks]

Your answers could include some of the following points.

1. *Romeo and Juliet*
- Juliet's impatience with the Nurse – references to time and age.
- Use of soliloquy – her thoughts jumping about – use of caesura.
- Personification of love and allusions to classical mythology.
- Imagery of light and dark.
- Her dependence on the Nurse, reflecting social context.

2. *Macbeth*
- He sees power as good and desirable – 'happy prologues'.
- He immediately has doubts because of the source of the prophecy.
- Use of soliloquy and rhetorical questions.
- The 'horrid' image is the idea of killing the king to gain power.
- The prophecy has a physical effect on him.

3. *The Tempest*
- Ariel is a slave. He is loyal to Prospero but wants to hold him to his bargain.
- Prospero reacts angrily to mention of Ariel's 'freedom'.
- Use of questions, exclamations and caesura to show this.
- Prospero treats Ariel like a naughty child. Father/child relationship?
- Prospero feels Ariel is indebted to him and has to be reminded of his past.

4. *Twelfth Night*
- Difference in social status/gender.
- In spite of this Maria tells him how to behave – but in an affectionate way.
- They are both dependent on Olivia.
- They are friendly and have an easy relationship.
- They plot together to use Sir Andrew.

5. *Henry V*
- His immediate reaction is calm and amused.
- He develops the metaphor of the tennis balls, turning it against the Dauphin.
- He stresses his status as king, using 'we'.
- Change of tone as he displays anger.
- Use of rhetorical language, e.g. repetition.

6. *The Merchant of Venice*
- He is protective to the point of locking her up.
- There is no evidence of any affection between them.
- When she elopes he seems more concerned with the money she has stolen.
- Her giving of the ring for a monkey indicates how little respect she has for him.
- The audience's sympathies might change.

7. *Julius Caesar*
- Cassius persuades Brutus to join the conspiracy.
- Cassius seems to have a personal grudge against Caesar.
- He describes him as physically weak and tells a story to prove it.
- Brutus is more interested in principles. He wants to defend Rome rather than attack Caesar.
- Caesar is shocked by Brutus's action ('Et tu, Brute?').

8. *Much Ado About Nothing*
- She is ambivalent about marriage.
- She is witty and opinionated and happy to express her opinions to men.
- She does not like being told what to do – but the less assertive Hero can trick her.
- She has a strong sense of justice and family loyalty.
- She is dependent on her uncle.

9. *Othello*
- Differences in age and race – the opposition of her father.
- Her admiration for him and his wooing with stories.
- Her innocence and naivety.

- His growing jealousy – his feelings are manipulated by Iago.
- Their deaths and how love leads to tragedy.

Page 69 Quick Test
1. False.   2. False.   3. True.
4. True.
Page 71 Quick Test
1. Yes.   2. An image or idea that recurs in a text.   3. Yes.   4. Yes.
Page 73 Quick Test
No definitive answer – check your notes.
Page 75 Quick Test
1. A variation of English spoken in a particular region.   2. The language of conversation.   3. An object that represents an idea or feeling.   4. Part of the story that takes place at an earlier time.

For mark scheme, see table for questions on pages 66–67. Your answers could include some of the following points.

1. *Julius Caesar*
- He starts with an oath ('Ye gods') to express the strength of his feelings.
- He compares Caesar to the Colossus, describing his power in terms of physical size.
- He uses words like 'petty' and 'dishonourable' to emphasize that Caesar is 'great' only because others let him be.
- He argues against the idea that we are controlled by fate.
- He insists that Caesar is no better than anyone else, using two rhetorical questions.

2. *Much Ado About Nothing*
- Beatrice's tone is light-hearted, although she is talking about a serious matter.
- She feels that she is different – 'Thus goes everyone to the world but I'.
- She flirts with Don Pedro, making a joke from the double meaning of 'get' to imply that she would like to marry him.
- She uses the metaphor of clothes to express the difference in status between her and Don Pedro.
- The last line sums up her ambiguous attitude to life.

3. *The Merchant of Venice*
- Shylock is anxious about Jessica as he had asked for news of her.
- However, he is more concerned about the money she has spent than her whereabouts.
- This is what the Elizabethan audience might expect from a Jew. Modern audiences might think such a stereotype was anti-Semitic.
- The metaphor 'Thou stick'st a dagger in me' suggests pain.
- The revelation about the ring changes our perception again.

4. *Othello*
- They have defied convention and prejudice by marrying – as her husband, Othello takes control.
- She cannot see the point of being married if she does not live with her husband.
- She uses religious language ('consecrate') to describe their love.
- She has fallen in love with his reputation as a soldier.
- The caesura in the last line of her speech emphasizes her determination.

5. *Romeo and Juliet*
- Their use of a sonnet suggests mutual love.
- Religious imagery could show the love to be sacred or could suggest it is sacrilegious.
- Juliet takes control and makes conditions, wanting to be sure.
- References to 'the stars' suggest their tragedy is inevitable.

- Although the audience's sympathies are with the couple, some could feel they are in the wrong when they defy their parents.

6. *Macbeth*
- Macbeth starts off loyal and happy with his status, but the meeting with the witches gives him ideas.
- His soliloquies show us he is ambitious for power but has a conscience.
- Lady Macbeth taunts him and pushes him into killing Duncan.
- When he gains power he cannot enjoy it because of his conscience and his feelings of vulnerability.
- He commits terrible acts to keep power, abuses power and ruins his country.

7. *The Tempest*
- Ariel is shown doing things that humans cannot, unseen by most characters.
- Prospero tells the story of how he freed Ariel from Sycorax.
- Ariel is contrasted with Caliban. They can be seen as two parts of humanity, or as two ways of being a slave.
- Ariel obeys Prospero and is rewarded with his freedom.
- An interest in discovery and colonization is reflected in Prospero and Ariel's relationship.

8. *Twelfth Night*
- They are responsible for the anarchy associated with Twelfth Night.
- Maria helps Sir Toby in his schemes and tries to control him.
- They provide broad comedy and a comic sub-plot, though their practical jokes can be seen as cruel.
- The audience might sympathize with Malvolio when he becomes a victim.
- They help to complicate the plot and confuse matters.

9. *Henry V*
- Henry is seen as a rightful, anointed king.
- He is clever politically, e.g. using the Dauphin's insult as an excuse to invade France.
- He seeks the approval of the church for what he does.
- He is an effective war leader, leading from the front bravely and planning well.
- He uses rhetoric to inspire loyalty and affection.

For mark scheme, see answers to questions on pages 66–67. Your answers could include some of the following points.

1. *The Strange Case of Dr Jekyll and Mr Hyde*
- The extract is in the third person but through the eyes of a maid, distancing it from the narrator.
- The old man has 'an innocent and old-world kindness', contrasting with the cruelty of the attacker.
- There is some mystery about why he has 'accosted' Hyde in the street.
- The violence builds over a few sentences – from impatiently playing with the cane. to attacking him with the cane.
- The expression 'ape-like fury' makes him seem inhuman.

2. *A Christmas Carol*
- Scrooge thinks the poor are being taken care of and it is none of his business.
- The gentleman reminds us that caring about others is central to Christmas and Christianity.
- His manner is abrupt and aggressive.
- His language is quite extreme and shocking. He thinks of people as just statistics.
- At the end he sets out his philosophy, using the double meaning of 'business'.

3. *Pride and Prejudice*
- The incident is seen through the eyes of Elizabeth so the impression we get is the same as hers.
- The conversation is a private one with his friend, so we can take it to be his true feelings.
- He is contrasted with Bingley, who is enjoying dancing and is very sociable.
- His language makes him sound very snobbish and when Bingley suggests he dance with Elizabeth, he shows himself to be bad-mannered.
- He damns Elizabeth with faint praise, calling her 'tolerable; but not handsome enough to tempt me'.

4. *Great Expectations*
- Pip's question about London being 'wicked' implies an assumption made by people outside London.
- However, he says it 'for the sake of saying something', which implies that he is not concerned or nervous.
- It seems as if Wemmick is more concerned about danger than Pip is.
- Mr Wemmick paints a picture of an amoral city.
- Most of the extract is in dialogue, without much comment. We know nothing about Wemmick and, like Pip, do not know whether to take notice of his opinions.

5. *The War of the Worlds*
- The first-person narrator describes events as he sees them, creating suspense.
- He has prior knowledge of astronomy and of what has happened on Mars.
- There is a sense of scientific curiosity about his reaction and he uses scientific terminology, as if writing an academic paper.
- There is a sense of calm, with none of the fear or panic of later chapters.
- The other onlookers are also curious, treating it as a day out.

6. *Frankenstein*
- The description of the monster is horrifying, who does not see beyond his appearance.
- Frankenstein is concerned about his safety and that of those he loves.
- The monster's actions are horrifying and Frankenstein feels both guilt and hatred.
- The monster can be seen as representing part of Frankenstein.
- His feelings change when the monster is given his own narrative, as do the feelings of the reader.

7. *The Sign of Four*
- Holmes draws conclusions from seemingly trivial evidence, showing wide and detailed knowledge.
- Watson's narrative puts the reader in Watson's place.
- Holmes always keeps something back from Watson, teasing the reader.
- In his use of forensics he is ahead of his time and ahead of the police.
- He is set apart from other people. His distrust of women and his drug-taking suggest a mysterious past.

8. *Jane Eyre*
- The relationship between employer and governess is odd. She is neither a servant nor a family member.
- Jane and Rochester both seem to 'earn' each other's love.
- The fire and the discovery of Bertha turn her world upside down. She has been lied to and betrayed.
- Symbolism and imagery are important. Rochester's blindness might signify that he can finally see the truth.
- At the end Jane is in control. She needs Rochester to be weakened in order to truly love him.

9. *Silas Marner*
- At the beginning Godfrey's story is separate from Silas's. They come together later.
- Godfrey's decisions are influenced more by status than by morality.
- He is portrayed sympathetically and we are given access to his thoughts.
- He is weak and irresponsible. Eliot is critical of his reliance on luck to get him out of trouble and his reluctance to deal with problems.
- He cannot understand why Eppie would not want to be adopted by him.

Pages 80–87 Revise Questions

Page 81 Quick Test
1. True. 2. True. 3. False.
4. True.
Page 83 Quick Test
All of them.
Page 85 Quick Test
1. Protagonist. 2. Narrator.
3. Dialogue. 4. Stage direction.
Page 87 Quick Test
1. Yes. 2. An act.
3. Where he/she comes from. 4. No.

Pages 88–89 Review Questions

For mark scheme, see answers to questions on pages 66–67. Your answers could include some of the following points.

1. *Frankenstein*
- The time – 'a dreary night of November' – sets the tone. The description could be seen as pathetic fallacy.
- His feelings are almost physical ('agony') and give us a feeling of dread.
- He has tried to create a man but describes him as a 'creature' and a 'thing'.
- His feelings are implied by his description, using adjectives like 'horrid', 'shrivelled' and 'dun'.
- The first-person narrative makes us see the experience as Frankenstein sees it.

2. *The Sign of Four*
- The narrator, Watson, is in the same position as the reader, waiting for Holmes to act and speak.
- Holmes sees the meaning of the footprints but does not share his conclusions with Watson, challenging him to 'try a little analysis'.
- He measures and examines things, showing that his detection is based on science.
- A simile, 'like…a trained bloodhound', is used to show his keenness and his sensitivity.
- He is confident about his conclusions – 'Why, we have got him, that's all.'

3. *Jane Eyre*
- Jane comes to his aid. He is the master, but due to his fall he is in a weak position.
- Jane is the narrator, so we see what she sees and she shares her feelings with us.
- She does not fall for his looks but points out that he is not handsome or young and mocks her own 'theoretical reverence' for good looks.
- At the same time she sees this as something they have in common, because she sees herself as unattractive.
- Fire and lightning might be associated with passion. Does she want to avoid sexual passion?

4. *Silas Marner*
- Godfrey reacts to Dunsey with 'an active expression of hatred'.
- Dunsey is just as antagonistic, his dislike increased by Godfrey's being the elder and more favoured brother.
- While Godfrey is described as good-natured and well-meaning, Dunsey is sarcastic and a lazy drunk.
- They are both dependent on their father. Godfrey is worried about his reactions.
- It is clear that Dunsey has the upper hand in the relationship. He knows Godfrey's secret and is using it to blackmail him.

5. *The Strange Case of Dr Jekyll and Mr Hyde*
- Most events take place in the dark or half-light.
- The multiple narratives mean that the story is 'distanced' from us. Truth is revealed gradually, the sealed letters adding to the suspense.
- Many elements are typical of the Gothic tradition.
- The narrators are logical, professional men, so they are sceptical. If they are afraid, it must be something awful.
- The physical descriptions of Hyde make him seem almost animal-like.

6. *A Christmas Carol*
- In the first chapter (Stave), he is seen as having no interest in family nor in society in general.
- The Ghost of Christmas Past is used to show how Scrooge became like he is, gaining some sympathy for him.
- The Ghost of Christmas Present takes the idea of 'other people' beyond family and acquaintances, showing Scrooge that he cannot cut himself off from the world.
- The Ghost of Christmas Yet to Come shows the result of his attitudes.
- Other characters are used as a contrast with Scrooge, showing love and the 'spirit of Christmas'.

7. *Pride and Prejudice*
- Darcy and Lady Catherine de Burgh are the highest-status characters in the novel. Her attitudes are seen as being shared by him.
- Some of his 'pride' could be reserve – perhaps the result of his class or of his nature.
- Those who know him best do not see him as proud, while those who criticize him, like Wickham, are not reliable.
- He is concerned about his reputation and that of his family, which can be seen as proud.
- His actions, especially with regard to Wickham, show his true nature.

8. *Great Expectations*
- Pip as narrator. Is he naive? Is he unreliable? The novel as a 'Bildungsroman'. Pip makes mistakes but learns from his experiences.
- His 'expectations' change him and he is seduced by money and false friends.
- His changing relationship with Joe shows how much he is changing, for the worse and then for the better.
- Dickens uses the Magwitch story to show Pip taking control and acting as an adult.
- His changing emotions towards Estella reflect a growing maturity.

9. *The War of the Worlds*
- Initially humans are not afraid of the Martians, which leads them into danger. Lack of fear, combined with ignorance, can mean lack of action.
- Fear is contagious. Some people help each other but most become selfish and even violent.
- Fear causes some people to act irrationally, but others, like the narrator, think logically.
- The curate questions his faith and goes mad; the narrator kills the curate to save himself.
- The narrator and the artilleryman face their fears and plan for the future.

Pages 90–91 Practice Questions

Give yourself 2 marks for each valid point supported by appropriate evidence. The points below are just suggestions. There are many other valid points to be made.

1. *An Inspector Calls*
- He comes from the 'future' so has the benefit of hindsight.
- He acts like a real detective, trying to solve a crime.
- However, he seems more interested in the other characters' attitudes to Eva – and is it really a crime that would be investigated?

- He is the mouthpiece for the writer, with his speech about the 'future'.
- He sometimes shows his impatience with the responses he gets.

2. *Blood Brothers*
- She is unhappy because she cannot have a baby, and it's her idea to take one of the babies.
- She seems to be aware that it will end tragically once Edward meets Mickey.
- Her wanting to get away from Mickey looks like snobbery but she is frightened of the secret getting out.
- She has mental health problems, maybe as a result of the secret.
- Her actions precipitate the tragic outcome.

3. *The History Boys*
- He could be seen as the leader of the group – others look up to him.
- He has an amoral attitude to sex. He is aware of his own attraction and quite vain – he uses it to bestow favours.
- His language can be very crude but he can also be eloquent.
- He does not understand why he is attracted to Irwin – although he himself sees everything in sexual terms, it is probably something else.
- He realizes that he enjoys having power and using it.

4. *DNA*
- She talks constantly in a 'stream of consciousness' style, giving access to her thoughts.
- She comments on what's been going on 'off-stage', giving us an insight into developments.
- She is discovering a lot of things for the first time and finds the world full of wonder.
- What is the meaning of her revelation that she killed her pet?
- What is the point of her relationship/non-relationship with Phil?

5. *The Curious Incident of the Dog in the Night-Time*
- He is 'different'. Many people would call him 'autistic' but this is not specifically mentioned.
- He takes things literally and speaks mostly of facts. He does not describe or speculate.
- The audience knows only what he knows, so we discover things with him.
- He proves to himself and others that he can cope, but in his own way.
- Is he the victim or the cause of his family's problems?

6. *A Taste of Honey*
- Her relationship with her mother is central – there is an element of role-reversal in it.
- In some ways she is mature for her age and in others naive.
- She might be seen as typical of a girl of her age and class at the time, but her circumstances are unusual.
- She is witty and honest, and shows signs of creativity.
- Through her eyes we see a world that is quite prejudiced and repressive, but she is not part of it.

7. *Hobson's Choice*
- His entrance from the cellar and expectation of a blow.
- His worth as a worker recognized by Mrs Hepworth and Hobson's contrasting attitude to him.
- Maggie's realization of his worth and potential.
- His shyness and the comic portrayal of his attitude to Maggie.
- He learns to stand up to Hobson and to Maggie.

8. *Journey's End*
- Context – his age and background typical of officers in the First World War.
- Public school background and attitudes apparent in his speech and references.

- The strain of responsibility as well as of war, leading to reliance on alcohol.
- Raleigh's 'hero worship' and Osborne's protective attitude.
- His revelations about his fears.

9. *My Mother Said I Never Should*
- Her role as daughter, mother and grandmother.
- Typical (stereotypical) woman of her time – keen to marry/romantic/suburban.
- Sense of frustration – limitations of role.
- Her adoption of Rosie and the change in her relationship with Jackie.
- Sense of self-sacrifice for others, e.g. taking on Rosie, not telling others about her illness.

10. *Lord of the Flies*
- Simon is inherently good: gentle and kind to the little 'uns.
- He has the same background as the other boys but, in his case, morality and civilization are not superficial.
- He sees what the 'beast' means.
- His hallucinations are almost mystical and holy.
- His murder represents the triumph of evil and savagery. He can be seen as a sacrificial victim, perhaps like Jesus.

11. *Telling Tales*
- Carla is the narrator, so we see things through her eyes.
- She is a person people do not really notice, so she can observe things without being part of them.
- She tells her story in a straightforward way, as if telling it to a friend.
- She is conscious of her status – not being a teacher – and keeps it from Steve.
- Her friendship with Steve helps her rediscover that part of her identity.

12. *Animal Farm*
- Boxer represents the honest working class, exploited by others.
- He is hard-working and loyal – first to Mr Jones, and then to the pigs.
- His naivety and trusting nature mean he is easily exploited.
- He is drawn sympathetically, though some readers might find him dull and frustrating.
- His death illustrates how little regard the pigs have for other animals.

13. *Never Let Me Go*
- Tommy's fits of temper and lack of 'creativity' mark him out as different.
- He does not actively rebel but he does not seem able to conform.
- For most of the novel Kathy does not understand his attitude but (unlike Ruth) she listens to him.
- He is interested in finding out about the 'gallery' before Kathy is.
- His value to society is only as a donor – but he inspires friendship and love in Kathy.

14. *Anita and Me*
- Anita could be seen as an antagonist, in some ways the opposite of the protagonist, Meena.
- The changes in Meena's attitude to her show that Meena is growing up.
- She represents the white working-class culture of Tollington.
- Her troubled family helps to make her more sympathetic.
- Her association with Sam brings the community's racism into focus.

15. *Pigeon English*
- He is protagonist and narrator. Is he a reliable narrator?
- His narration resembles a diary; its tone is chatty and colloquial.
- His speech reflects his age and background.
- He is keen to 'solve' the murder, not realizing the danger he is in.
- His innocence leads him to see things in a positive light, treating most of life as a game, although he is in a very dangerous environment.

16. *The Woman in Black*
- His position as a lawyer and his careful, thorough manner suggest he is a reliable narrator.
- In the first chapter he tells us how his experiences changed him.
- Emphasizes his scepticism but has a sense of adventure.
- He does not want to appear weak or superstitious and tries to ignore 'hints' about Eel Marsh House.
- He is romantic, sensitive and sympathetic.

17. *Oranges Are Not the Only Fruit*
- She can be seen as Jeanette's antagonist: her presence dominates the novel.
- Her faith is strong, evangelical and genuine. Everything she does and says is informed by religion.
- She has plans for Jeanette and makes her what she is.
- Her attitude to sex and sexuality.
- Jeanette, the narrator's feelings about her and what she stands for.

Page 93 Quick Test
1. False.   2. False.   3. True.
4. True.

Page 95 Quick Test
1. Yes.   2. Yes.   3. Yes.   4. No.

Page 97 Quick Test
1. Onomatopoeia.   2. Personification.
3. Alliteration.   4. Persona.

Page 99 Quick Test
1. Rhyming couplet.   2. Internal rhyme.
3. Ballad.   4. Free verse.

Page 101 Quick Test
1. Similarity.   2. Difference.
3. Difference.   4. Similarity.

Give yourself 2 marks for each valid point supported by appropriate evidence. The points below are just suggestions. There are many other valid points to be made.

1. *An Inspector Calls*
- At the time the play is set, women did not have the vote.
- Eva represents different things in different people's eyes. Their ideas are shaped by gender and class.
- Mrs Birling fulfils the expected role of a middle-class wife.
- Sheila seems to do little but shop and get engaged – but she finds a voice at the end.
- There is a double standard in terms of sexual morality.

2. *Blood Brothers*
- By starting with a tableau of the end, Russell shows the tragedy is inevitable.
- Mrs Johnstone is very superstitious.
- Mrs Lyons does not believe in superstitions at first but becomes obsessed by escaping from fate.
- The narrator speaks about fate.
- The characters might think their lack of choice is because of fate, but is it the consequence of their actions or the result of economics and politics?

3. *The History Boys*
- Double/triple meaning in title – are the boys making history as well as studying history? Could this have happened only in the past?
- Mrs Lintott's approach to history is conventional and designed to equip pupils to pass exams.
- Irwin wants them to question everything – a different way of looking at history, but his approach is also about passing exams.
- Irwin's idea that there is 'no need to tell the truth' can be applied to history, politics and life in general.
- Irwin ends up playing a part in history as a political adviser.

4. *DNA*
- When they think they are guilty of a crime, their reaction is to avoid blame.
- Some of the teenagers are nervous and scared but do not really accept their responsibility.
- They tend to look for 'leaders' to absolve them from responsibility.
- They frame the innocent postman. They have no qualms about this.
- Later they plan the actual murder of Adam. By this time some of them have drifted off. Only Leah objects.

5. *The Curious Incident of the Dog in the Night-Time*
- Christopher's family is unusual, as he lives with his widowed father. The audience would probably admire his father.
- Our perceptions are changed when we find Ed has lied and Judy is alive.
- Christopher does not like physical contact and does not express emotion. He does not realize this is a problem.
- We see the strain this has put on his parents in different ways.
- Judy's letters give an account of a happier family, as well as explaining her point of view about the difficulties of family life.

6. *A Taste of Honey*
- Helen is not interested in love. She marries Peter for a comfortable life.
- Jo's relationship with the Boy seems romantic, yet she is not bothered about his not coming back.
- The only relationship that seems loving is with her homosexual friend Geof. Maybe she cannot connect love and sex.
- The central relationship is that between Jo and Helen – a 'love–hate' relationship.
- Jo's relationships are all unconventional for the time, but the play is part of the fashion for 'kitchen sink drama', trying to show 'real life' on the stage.

7. *Hobson's Choice*
- The importance of marriage to women: Vickey and Alice anxious to get married while Maggie is 'on the shelf'.
- Vickey's and Alice's relationships are conventional, their fiancés respectable, while Maggie's choice is seen as unsuitable.
- Her courtship of him is equally unconventional and is treated comically.
- Maggie sees marriage as a business venture and has no time for sentiment.
- However, there proves to be real love between Maggie and Willie.

8. *Journey's End*
- There is a constant sense of danger outside the bunker.
- Usually the characters do not discuss feelings but focus on everyday matters.
- This reflects their background, as do their references to school and sport.
- Hibbert's expression of his fear is shocking, Stanhope's reaction showing the importance of discipline.

- Stanhope's revelations of his own fears and how he deals with them.

9. *My Mother Said I Never Should*
- The role of mother changes with society but for Doris and Margaret it is their main role.
- Margaret claims not to want children but Jackie becomes her main focus. There is ambiguity in her attitude.
- Why does Jackie give up Rosie? She is not coping but she does not persevere.
- Is she making a reasonable choice, putting her career first, or is she shirking responsibility?
- Rosie's reaction to learning Jackie is her mother.

10. *Lord of the Flies*
- The boys' background suggests they are the epitome of Western civilization, so their savagery is shocking.
- They seek organization and order at first, but they are constructing an idea of order.
- Strong leadership emerges in the form of Jack, showing that the idea of 'leadership' as a force for good is misplaced.
- Civilization is a thin veneer. Our instincts are to be savage, even evil. The beast is a symbol of savagery.
- The breakdown of 'civilization' on the island is no worse than the wars being fought by the apparently civilized world.

11. *Telling Tales*
- The reality of death is ever-present. Accidental deaths in the mines are not uncommon.
- Walter's mother is distraught at his death, while his wife seems to feel little emotion.
- The bringing in and laying out of the body are described in detail, giving a sense of the physicality of death.
- The chrysanthemums are symbolic, their significance changing.
- Elizabeth has to 'submit' to life and carry on but she is now aware that death is her 'ultimate master'.

12. *Animal Farm*
- The animals escape one form of oppression only to find another.
- They allow the pigs to change into oppressors by looking to them for leadership and naively trusting them.
- The pigs use slogans and songs, and manipulate language in order to oppress the other animals.
- The oppressors depend on spies and traitors to survive.
- *Animal Farm* is based on the events after the Russian Revolution but it is a 'fable' and its lessons can be applied to all kinds of oppressive regimes.

13. *Never Let Me Go*
- The novel centres on Kathy's friendship with Ruth and Tommy, seen through her eyes.
- Friendship may be more important to them because they do not have families.
- Their friendships are in many ways like those of any teenagers and young adults, but they are more intense because of their being kept apart.

- Friendships often turn into sexual relationships. People want to be part of a couple.
- The relationship between carer and donor is a form of friendship – Kathy is allowed to choose her donors.

14. *Anita and Me*
- As there are no other non-white children, Meena keeps her culture separate.
- Differences in culture are shown in dress and in food.
- Meena wants to belong and acts like the other children, exaggerating her accent to be accepted.
- Nanima brings Meena closer to her Punjabi culture. She is protective of her grandmother and, by implication, her culture.
- Meena becomes aware of racism as she matures. When the novel ends she moves away from Tollington and further into her Punjabi culture.

15. *Pigeon English*
- The novel focuses on the repercussions of a single violent act – a boy's murder.
- Harri is fascinated by the murder and tries to investigate it, treating it as an adventure rather than a dangerous reality.
- The school and area are dominated by gangs. Violence and petty crime seem to be part of everyday life.
- Harri's aunt has committed an act of violence on herself.

16. *The Woman in Black*
- The narrator is initially unwilling to believe in the supernatural.
- The remote location and descriptions of landscape and weather create atmosphere.
- The reactions of local people suggest the presence of the supernatural.
- Arthur's attempts to rationalize his experiences are unsuccessful.
- Arthur comes to understand what is happening but has no power against evil forces.

17. *Oranges Are Not the Only Fruit*
- Being adopted sets Jeanette apart from others. Her mother sees her as a possession, a gift from God.
- The church gives Jeanette a sense of identity but her religion sets her apart from other children.
- The stories of Perceval and Winnet express her need to belong.
- Her lesbianism results in her being rejected by church and family.
- She seems to embrace being different from others.

Pages 104–105 **Practice Questions**

For all questions look at the mark scheme below, decide which description is closest to your answer and then decide which mark to give yourself.

Marks	Skills
18–20	• You have compared texts in an exploratory and critical way. • You have used precise, appropriate references to support your interpretation. • You have analysed the writer's methods using subject terminology appropriately. • You have explored the effects of the writer's methods. • You have explored links between text and ideas/context.
15–17	• You have made thoughtful, developed comparisons. • You have used appropriate references to support your interpretation. • You have examined the writer's methods using subject terminology effectively. • You have examined the effects of the writer's methods. • You have thoughtfully considered links between text and ideas/context.
11–14	• You have made clear comparisons. • You have used references effectively to support your explanation. • You have clearly explained the writer's methods using relevant subject terminology. • You have understood the effects of the writer's methods. • You have clearly understood links between text and ideas/context.

[Maximum 20 marks]

1. Your answer might include:
    - Ideas about who is affected by conflict and how – soldiers, relatives, civilians.
    - Comparisons dealing with soldiers during and after the conflict: 'The Charge of the Light Brigade', 'Bayonet Charge', 'Exposure', 'Remains'.
    - Comparisons of the effect on non-combatants: 'Poppies', 'The Émigrée', 'War Photographer'.
    - Use of alliteration, imagery and descriptions of nature.
    - Use of the speaker to explore ideas and context.
2. Your answer might include:
    - Ideas about what love means – 'I think of thee!', 'When We Two Parted', 'Winter Swans'.
    - Different stages in love; the beginning and the end – 'Neutral Tones', 'Singh Song!', 'When We Two Parted'.
    - The use of imagery of nature.
    - Direct address to the loved one.
    - Structure of a logical argument.
3. Your answer might include:
    - Lasting/intense love – 'The Manhunt', 'She Walks in Beauty'.
    - Direct address to the subject – 'A Complaint', 'Neutral Tones', 'I wanna be yours'.
    - Petrarchan sonnet – use of strict rhyme and metre and logical construction.
    - Use of imagery.
    - Use of writer's personal experience.
4. Your answer might include:
    - A strong, ballad-like story, with a regular pattern of rhyme and metre – 'The Charge of the Light Brigade'.

- Conflict in the family – 'Catrin'.
- Bitterness and resentment – 'A Poison Tree'.
- The speaker feels like an outsider, unfairly rejected – 'Half-caste', 'The Class Game', 'No Problem'.
- Ends with a sense of triumph/pride – 'The Class Game', 'No Problem'.
5. Your answer might include:
    - Description of a specific place – 'London', 'Stewart Island'.
    - Nostalgic mood – 'Absence', 'Home Thoughts from Abroad', 'Where the Picnic Was'.
    - Regular rhyme scheme / structured in four quatrains.
    - Regularity of metre broken up by caesura in first two stanzas: sense of stopping and starting.
    - Literal imagery describing nature – 'To Autumn', 'Home Thoughts from Abroad'.
6. Your answer might include:
    - Bereavement and absence – 'Love after Love', 'A Broken Appointment', 'The Sorrow of True Love'.
    - Lasting love – 'An Arundel Tomb', 'The Sorrow of True Love'.
    - Literal imagery of everyday things – 'Dusting the Phone', 'Love after Love'.
    - Linking of parents' love for each other with son's love.
    - Regularity of structure and form.
    - Change from third to second person at the end.
7. Your answer might include:
    - Focus on the ordinary soldier in war – 'Vergissmeinnicht', 'The Man He Killed'.

- Strong, shocking imagery to describe victims – 'Punishment', 'The Destruction of Sennacherib'.
- Sense of pointlessness of war – 'Vergissmeinnicht', 'Flag', 'The Man He Killed'.
- Use of sounds: alliteration/onomatopoeia.
- Description of 'normal' funeral rites to contrast with the soldiers' deaths.
- Tone of mourning and sorrow.
8. Your answer might include:
    - Focus on childhood innocence – 'Spring and Fall: to a Young Child', 'Midnight on the Great Western'.
    - Children in the care of adults or uncared for / in danger – 'Red Roses', 'Out, Out'. Irony in the description of the 'guardians'?
    - Describes a real event and considers what it means – 'Cold Knap Lake', 'Midnight on the Great Western'.
    - Use of imagery associated with innocence: lambs and flowers – 'The Bluebell', 'Red Roses'.
    - Regular rhyme and metre, with long lines (heptameters) reflecting the lines of children.
9. Your answer might include:
    - The power and violence of nature – 'Hawk Roosting', 'The Prelude'.
    - Growing up (an epiphany) – 'The Prelude'.
    - The imagery of war – 'Mametz Wood', 'Dulce et Decorum Est'.
    - Change in attitude to the frogs through the poem.
    - Language – contrast of the poet's language and the babyish language of the teacher.
    - Use of sounds: onomatopoeia, alliteration, rhyme.

Pages 106–107 Review Questions

1. a) A persona. An old mother.
    b) In a house, probably in a poor rural area, during the course of a day.
    c) Yes. There are four stressed syllables per line, though the number of unstressed syllables varies. The regularity could reflect the routine of her day. In spite of her hard life, it gives the poem a cheerful tone.
    d) Yes. It is in rhyming couplets, regular and simple, reflecting a regular and simple life.
    e) Mostly, it is literal, describing what she sees, though the fire could be taken as a metaphor for life and the stars are personified as they 'blink and peep'.
    f) It is the story of an ordinary old woman's day and her life.
    g) Fire could be a symbol of life. Growing feeble and then cold is an image for old age.
    h) Old age. A woman's role. Death. Work. Envy of the young.
    i) He feels sympathy for the old woman. He sees life as pointless. He is saddened by the passing of time.
    j) All answers are valid.
    [2 marks for each point]

2. Look at the mark scheme below, decide which description is closest to your answer and then decide which mark to give yourself.

Marks	Skills
18–20	• You have explored the texts critically. • You have used precise references to support your interpretation. • You have analysed the writers' methods using appropriate subject terminology. • You have explored the effects of the writers' methods on the reader. • You have explored comparisons of the writers' use of language, structure and form, using appropriate subject terminology. • You have convincingly compared the effects of the writers' methods on the reader.
15–17	• You have responded thoughtfully to the texts. • You have used appropriate references to support your interpretation. • You have examined the writers' methods using subject terminology effectively. • You have examined the effects of the writers' methods on the reader. • You have thoughtfully compared the writers' use of language and/or structure and/or form, using effective subject terminology. • You have thoughtfully compared the effects of the writers' methods on the reader.
11–14	• You have responded clearly to the texts. • You have used references effectively to support your explanation. • You have explained the writers' methods using relevant subject terminology. • You have understood the effects of the writers' methods on the reader. • You have clearly compared the writers' use of language and/or structure and/or form, using effective subject terminology. • You have clearly compared the effects of the writers' methods on the reader.

Your answer might include comments on:
- Clare's entirely positive view of nature / Tennyson's focus on nature's power.
- Repetition of 'I love'.
- Use of the sonnet form for a poem about nature.
- Hope and joy brought about by the season.
- Use of personification.

- Listing of all aspects of nature in 'Sonnet' – animals, plants, the weather.
- The lack of punctuation, giving a sense of freedom, in 'Sonnet'.
- Use of alliteration and onomatopoeia to create sounds.
- Presence of speaker.
- Differences in structure.
[Maximum 20 marks]

1. 'Unfit for active service'. **[1]**   2. The trams come off the rails. **[1]** The trams catch fire. **[1]**   3. b. **[1]**
4. See 'Skills' column of table on page 129 (for pages 34–35 Practice Questions, Q2).

Marks	Examples of possible content
7–8	The writer writes at first as if he is explaining something to us, describing in detail something that is happening now. The phrase 'the spirit of the devil' makes us think of evil, and the descriptions of darkness and flames might also have connotations of hell and damnation. Yet there is a sense of excitement in the extended metaphor of the horse race. The paragraph ends with a comic contrast between the danger of the fire and the passengers' down-to-earth colloquial reaction: 'We're stopping where we are. Push on, George.'
5–6	He writes in the present tense and we can imagine ourselves there. The metaphor of the 'steeple-chase' makes the tram seem like a living thing and the experience like being on a horse. There is a contrast between the 'blackness' and 'heart of nowhere', which sound ominous, and the cheerful speech of the people.

[Maximum 8 marks]

5. See 'Skills' column of table on page 131 (for pages 64–65 Review Questions, Q1).

Marks	Examples of possible content
7–8	The writer moves from the general to the particular. The first three paragraphs move from describing the trams as something exotic and fantastical to telling us about particular people on them. The mood changes at the start of paragraph 2 with 'The reason for this', which leads into an account of what the trams are actually used for, contrasting with the fantastical imagery of the first paragraph…
5–6	At first the focus is on the tram ride and how exciting it is, at the same time telling us about the setting. The focus shifts to the passengers and how they feel about the tram service – more of the reality of it. In the third paragraph he gives a general description of drivers and conductors. Then we have some dialogue, which brings the focus to one conductor, Annie.

[Maximum 8 marks]

6. See 'Skills' column of table on page 129 (for pages 34–35 Review Questions, Q2).

Marks	Examples of possible content
16–20	The writer only describes the men briefly, his main focus being the girl conductors. However, he gives a very vivid impression of the men in a few words. Although they are 'cripples and hunchbacks', who might be looked down on, especially because they are not at war, they have the 'spirit of the devil', a comparison which makes them seem exotic and exciting. The girls are introduced to us as 'fearless young hussies', implying that they do not behave in the way expected of women at the time. He goes on to compare them to non-commissioned officers. Coupled with a description of their unflattering uniform, this may not sound complimentary, but the tone of the description suggests admiration and respect…
11–15	At first the people who work on the trams sound like misfits and are described in a quite insulting way – 'cripples and hunchbacks', but then the writer says they have 'the spirit of the devil in them'. This could mean they are wicked but, from what he then says, I think he means they are reckless and brave. The girls are different because they would not be at war anyway. They are young and very confident. He calls them 'fearless young hussies', which makes them sound attractive but a bit frightening.

[Maximum 20 marks]

7. Look at the mark scheme on page 131 (for pages 54–55 Practice Questions, Q3). This task is marked for content and organization, and for technical accuracy.
[Maximum 40 marks]
8. b, d, f, g **[4]**
9. See 'Skills' column of table on page 129 (for pages 34–35 Review Questions, Q2).

Marks	Examples of possible content
10–12	In the first paragraph, Dickens uses images of light and richness to describe Florence: 'bright…glittering…like gold!' His exclamations and his use of the second person ('we') make us feel his wonder as if we were there with him. In the second paragraph, he moves into the city and his language reflects both the atmosphere and the architecture. He personifies the buildings, describing 'distrustful windows' and saying they 'frown, in their old sulky state'…
7–9	Dickens writes in the present tense and the first person ('we') as if he is telling us what happens as it happens. He describes the buildings as if they were people, saying they 'frown'. He contrasts the beautiful palaces with the prison, summing up how uncomfortable it is in the simile 'cells like ovens'.

[Maximum 12 marks]

10. See 'Skills' column of table on page 129 (for pages 34–35 Practice Questions, Q5).

Marks	Examples of possible content
7–8	Both writers say the city is beautiful. Dickens describes the view from outside the city and then the centre. Rackham describes tourist places, like the Ponte Vecchio, but says tourists are 'littering' it and also mentions graffiti and 'a very ugly souvenir stall'. Dickens does not say anything about other tourists. Rackham focuses on the tourist areas, whereas Dickens is more interested in the prison and its inmates.
5–6	Dickens is very impressed by the 'magnificent' city and describes its beauty. Rackham also describes some of the attractions but talks about graffiti and an 'ugly' stall. Dickens sees a negative side of the city but for him it is the prison, next to the great castle, and the violence of a place where 'they are all blood-stained'. According to Rackham, the downside of Florence is all the tourists, who are spoiling what they come to see.

[Maximum 8 marks]

11. See 'Skills' column of table on page 130 (for pages 54–55 Practice Questions, Q2).

Marks	Examples of possible content
13–16	Dickens is writing about his personal experience of visiting Florence and the effect it had on him, whereas the purpose of Rackham's article is to examine the 'dilemma' of a city dependent on tourists being ruined by 'mass tourism and potential speculators'. Dickens uses hyperbolic, poetic images to describe the city 'shining in the sun like gold' but also 'stern and sombre'. Rackham starts almost by imitating Dickens as she describes a statue looking 'sternly', but for her this implies a judgement on the tourists, and from then on her focus is not on describing the city but on the issues.
9–12	Rackham writes about the issues of tourism and pollution and their effect on the city. Dickens does not mention this, perhaps because it was not a problem in his day. He describes the 'magnificent' city in detail, whereas she just sketches in a few details about the shops on the Ponte Vecchio in order to show us the 'dilemma of contemporary Florence'.

[Maximum 16 marks]

12. Look at the mark scheme on page 130 (for pages 54–55 Practice Questions, Q3). This task is marked for content and organization, and for technical accuracy.
   [Maximum 40 marks]

Questions 13–21
For all questions look at the mark scheme below.

Marks	Skills
35–40	• You have responded to the task in an exploratory and critical way. • You have used precise, appropriate references to support your interpretation. • You have analysed the writer's language using subject terminology appropriately. • You have analysed the writer's use of form and structure using subject terminology appropriately. • You have explored the effects of the writer's methods. • You have explored links between text and ideas/context. • Your spelling, punctuation and grammar are of a consistently excellent standard.
28–34	• You have responded to the task in a thoughtful, developed way. • You have used appropriate references to support your interpretation. • You have examined the writer's language using subject terminology effectively. • You have examined the writer's use of form and structure using subject terminology effectively. • You have examined the effects of the writer's methods. • You have thoughtfully considered links between text and ideas/context. • Your spelling, punctuation and grammar are of a consistently high standard.
21–27	• You have responded to the task in a clear way. • You have used references effectively to support your explanation. • You have clearly explained the writer's language using relevant subject terminology. • You have clearly explained the writer's use of form and structure methods using relevant subject terminology. • You have understood the effects of the writer's methods. • You have clearly understood links between text and ideas/context. • Your spelling, punctuation and grammar are mostly accurate.

Your answers could include some of the following points:

13. *Julius Caesar*
* Antony's use of rhetorical language.
* His praise of Brutus and the conspirators.
* The way he seeks to portray himself as one of the people and his actions after he has got them on his side.
* His position as Caesar's protégé.
* His actions after he has got the people on his side.
* His dealings with Octavius and Lepidus.

14. *Much Ado About Nothing*
* Two meanings of honour – sexual reputation and the obligation to defend your reputation and that of your friends.
* Benedick knows Hero has been 'wronged' but he is not part of Hero's family so he is not obliged to defend her.
* 'A man's office' – different ideas of honour for men and women.
* Defending Hero's honour shows his love for Beatrice and shows that he understands 'honour' as being a matter of right and wrong, not loyalty.
* Honour is associated with the court and the aristocracy. Claudio has not acted as a man of his class should.

15. *Macbeth*
* Lady Macbeth takes control. She may be more ruthless, happy to blame the grooms.
* The knocking makes him nervous but she reacts in a practical way.
* Lady Macbeth persuades Macbeth to murder Duncan. She embraces evil; he knows he is doing wrong.
* He discusses his guilt but hers seems not to affect her until the sleepwalking scene.
* As a woman she can only have power through him, but she is dominant and taunts him about his role as a man.

16. *Romeo and Juliet*
* Imagery of light and dark is used to express Juliet's beauty, and religious imagery is introduced.
* The effect of the soliloquy while the ball continues around him.
* Comparison with his ideas about love in the first scene. Here, mutual love is expressed in a sonnet.
* Portrayal of his love and their relationship in the balcony scene.
* His commitment to her and his actions after their marriage.
* Association of love and death.

17. *The Tempest*
* Prospero's power over Miranda is increased by his use of magic.
* He is angry and not willing to listen, using her inexperience of the world to control her.
* He is protective. He may be jealous of Ferdinand and/or unwilling to see Miranda grow up.
* However, he is won over by their love and welcomes Ferdinand – part of the general reconciliation at the end.
* Magic is seen as part of Prospero's learning and his power.
* Good and evil magic – refer to Sycorax.

18. *The Merchant of Venice*
* Mercy seen as God-given and natural.
* Mercy contrasted with power, symbolized in the sceptre, but seen as necessary in a ruler.
* It is not the opposite of justice but 'seasons' it.
* Portia's use of rhetorical language to convince Shylock.
* The failure of her appeal to Shylock and what this says about him.
* Is the outcome of the trial just? Would differences in Elizabethan and modern attitudes influence an audience's reaction to the trial?

19. *Twelfth Night*
* Viola's use of the conditional – 'I would' – which is taken by Olivia to express her true feelings but, in fact, expresses her feelings for Orsino.
* Language of pain and sorrow – 'suff'ring', 'deadly'.
* She talks about wanting to be open and honest, which she cannot be.
* Viola takes on her brother's identity – they are one.
* Disguise leads to confusion between the sexes and comedy.
* Paradoxically, disguise can allow people to be more honest.

20. *Henry V*
* Use of rhetorical language, e.g. lists of three, hyperbole.
* Refers immediately to God, his only authority and the source of his power.
* Refers to himself in the third person ('your king') and the first person plural ('we'), asserting his superiority.
* Although he mentions mercy, he gives none, showing he can be ruthless.
* Consider speeches where he shows other qualities, e.g. how he inspires his men at Agincourt. He is seen as a war leader and successful king.
* More ordinary/human side seen in interactions with soldiers and wooing of Katherine.

21. *Othello*
* Although he is the villain, Shakespeare gives him soliloquies so we have access to his plans and motivation.
* This is in the medieval tradition of the Devil in mystery plays.
* There is no evidence that he is right about Othello and Emilia – but the rumour 'will do as if for surety'.
* The audience might think that he has other reasons, e.g. bitterness and jealousy.
* He is the opposite of Othello, who has a 'free and open nature', but Othello will prove as quick to believe his wife is unfaithful.
* Because of his soliloquies the audience is drawn into Iago's plans, but as they progress we see the effects of his dishonesty and ruthlessness.

Questions 22–30
See mark scheme for Shakespeare (above). Your answers could include some of the following points.

22. *Frankenstein*
* The monster's speech is calm, whereas we, like Frankenstein, might expect him to be aggressive.
* The monster is humble and even servile in his approach – 'I am thy creature'.
* He uses gentle language – 'mild', 'clemency' – contrasting with Frankenstein's violent language.
* He uses logic, and refers to ideas of justice and to the Bible, suggesting he is intelligent and educated.
* This chapter marks a turning point, leading to the monster's narration.
* His story shows the potential he had for good and how this was destroyed.

23. *The Sign of Four*
* Watson draws conclusions about her character, which do not have the logical basis of conclusions that Holmes might make.
* She is drawn as a sympathetic character and a victim who needs protecting.
* Her main purpose is to introduce the plot. The note she has been sent leads into the mystery and adventure.
* Her romance with Watson forms a sub-plot, which contrasts with the main plot.

- The reactions of Watson and Holmes to her differ sharply – Watson is shocked at Holmes's misogyny; Holmes lacks Watson's empathy.
- The reader might suspect that Watson is foolish in falling for her and she could be tricking him, but he is proved right.

24. *Jane Eyre*
- The passage starts with 'Unjust!' Jane feels that she does not belong and is used as a scapegoat.
- Even as a child, Jane does not conform to her expected role.
- The Red Room is a powerful symbol of isolation from society, which Jane refers to throughout the novel.
- The description of the room and the weather can be related to the Gothic tradition, although the supernatural elements are not real but the result of a child's fears.
- Jane looks for love and substitute families throughout the novel. Her position as governess is neither servant nor family.
- She thinks of herself as different – in her looks and her nature.

25. *Pride and Prejudice*
- Pemberley is described as elegant, tasteful and beautiful. This says something about its owner which surprises Elizabeth.
- The idea of being its mistress appeals to her – she would not marry just for money but wants a 'good' marriage.
- The housekeeper maintains he is not proud. She is seen as reliable and honest.
- The way he treats and reacts to Wickham are central to Elizabeth's changing feelings.
- We are given access to Elizabeth's feelings through Austen's narrative style.

26. *Great Expectations*
- The strangeness of the setting and the contrast between Miss Havisham and Estella.
- How Dickens describes Estella's appearance.
- Estella's attitude towards Pip and how far this is due to Miss Havisham. Pip's love for Estella in spite of this.
- Violence to women – Estella's marriage – Mrs Gargery's death.
- Joe's marriage to Pip's sister / his marriage to Biddy.
- Influence of 'mother figures' on the orphaned Pip.

27. The *Strange Case of Dr Jekyll and Mr Hyde*
- Utterson is introduced as a reliable, logical, professional man.
- His profession gives him access to Lanyon, Jekyll and their documents.
- Utterson and Enfield are 'dull', making the contrast with the events Enfield describes greater.
- Contrast between the 'thriving' street and 'sinister' building, like Jekyll and Hyde.
- Use of imagery to create atmosphere.
- Utterson is inquisitive but also discreet – information is gradually revealed to him.

28. *A Christmas Carol*
- The importance of family life and being with loved ones – contrast with Scrooge's situation.
- Dickens's characteristic use of lists to build descriptions of plenty and a sense of excitement and anticipation.
- Bob refers to Tiny Tim's words about Christ.
- A sense throughout the novel that celebration and caring for others go together.
- The ghost shows Scrooge a range of people celebrating Christmas.
- Dickens's use of a popular genre to put across a serious message about society.

29. *The War of the Worlds*
- The artilleryman expects the Martians to remain in power and has planned accordingly.
- He sees himself and people like him surviving by living in the wild.
- He expects others will become 'pets' of the Martians, or be used for breeding and food.

The Martians are seen as superior and humans as animals.
- His vision, though it seems cynical, is similar to what happens in many oppressive regimes.
- Wells shows humans resisting a superior power, panicking and being destroyed.
- The Martians are defeated by nature before we get to see whether the artilleryman is right.

30. *Silas Marner*
- There is a distinction made between religious belief and church practices.
- The church in Lantern Yard is attended by working-class people who have a simple faith.
- Their practices are different from the established church but they believe absolutely in them.
- Eliot portrays the drawing of lots as something only ignorant, uneducated people could believe in.
- Silas cannot distinguish between the church and God, leading him to reject God.
- Raveloe's community seem to have a more Christian spirit than Lantern Yard's, shown by the way they support Silas and Eppie.

Questions 31–47
See the mark scheme for Shakespeare (above).
Your answers could include some of the following points.

31. *An Inspector Calls*
- His physical presence and bombastic style of speech.
- His social position as a rich, self-made man.
- His views on politics, society and the future.
- His traditional role in the family and relations with his wife and children.
- His contact with Eva Smith and what it tells us about industrial relations.
- The difference hindsight makes to an assessment of his character (both from the 1940s and a modern perspective).

32. *Blood Brothers*
- Narrator comments on action.
- Narrator enters action as various minor characters, to comic effect.
- Narrator used to move story forward.
- Narrator's musings on fate, superstition etc.
- How the narrator becomes sinister.
- Does he control as well as comment on the action?

33. *The History Boys*
- Irwin as stereotypical young, keen supply teacher.
- Headmaster's use of Irwin to get results and to undermine Hector.
- Compare/contrast with Mrs Lintott and Hector.
- His disregard for the truth and the revelation that he lied about his background.
- His sexuality / interest in Dakin and comparisons with Hector's 'groping'.
- His use as a framing device to start the acts from the 'present'.

34. *DNA*
- Characters come mostly in pairs, in established friendships.
- Their action demands group loyalty.
- Reported sentimental outpouring of friendship and grief for the 'dead' boy. Contrast this with their responsibility and guilt.
- How friendships fall apart.
- How some are leaders and some followers – and how leadership of the group changes.
- What is meant by friendship? Is it meaningful in this context?

35. *The Curious Incident of the Dog in the Night-Time*
- Scenes between her and Christopher show how he reacts to others in school.
- She is a sounding board for Christopher's thoughts/ideas/plans.
- She reads out the letters and is therefore a channel through which we hear Judy's point of view.

There is sympathy but a lack of emotional attachment – this might make it easier for Christopher to deal with her.

36. *A Taste of Honey*
- Description of Helen as 'semi-whore' implies casual attitude to sex and society's disapproval.
- Helen more interested in money/security than love.
- Jo has grown up without the usual parental attitudes to sex of the period.
- Unlike Helen she does associate sex with love – she craves affection.
- Attitudes to pre-marital sex / single mothers and homosexuality then and now.

37. *Hobson's Choice*
- Maggie can be seen as a 'new woman', typical of the time the play was written.
- Vickey and Alice are happy with a more traditional role.
- Mrs Hepworth has power and influence because of her money.
- Generally, the women seem to be more in control than the men.
- In their marriage, Maggie and Willie at first reverse the traditional roles.
- Maggie helps Willie to get to the point where he can stand up to her. They become equals.

38. *Journey's End*
- The quotation refers to Raleigh's feelings about Stanhope.
- This 'hero-worship' has more to do with admiring an older boy at school than with war.
- Stanhope feels uncomfortable with the idea.
- He is concerned about not living up to his reputation and about Raleigh's sister finding out.
- Osborne, the former teacher, feels it has value and defends Raleigh.
- The play shows what 'heroism' in war is really like.

39. *My Mother Said I Never Should*
- None of the men are ever seen, so everything we know about them comes from the women.
- The women's lives are determined by their relationships with men.
- Doris and Margaret are forced to take secondary roles, supporting their husbands.
- They both seem to love their husbands but there is some resentment.
- Ken leaving Margaret seems almost random – to show men cannot be relied on?

40. *Lord of the Flies*
- The Lord of the Flies – the sow's head – symbolizing evil and lack of civilization. How they come to worship it – its association with the Devil through Beelzebub.
- Symbolism of the conch – democracy and civilization.
- The Beast – an imaginary thing that becomes a powerful symbol.
- Symbolism of place – the forest glade, the mountain, the beach, the island as a whole.
- Piggy's glasses, symbolizing intellect and reason, and the conch, symbolizing democracy and civilization, are both destroyed.
- How the meaning of symbols can change and/ or be ambiguous.

41. *Telling Tales*
- The narrator's version of his parents' happy family life and his interpretation of the relationship between Mother and Ralph.
- Tensions between narrator and Ralph / Grandfather and Ralph – competing for Mother's affection?
- Compare Mother's reaction to husband's death with 'The Darkness Out There' / 'The Odour of Chrysanthemums' / 'A Family Supper'.
- Narrative viewpoint – compare with 'My Polish Teacher's Tie' – unreliable/reliable viewpoint.
- Ideas about marriage – 'The Odour of Chrysanthemums', 'A Family Supper'.

- Use of symbolism and imagery – 'The Odour of Chrysanthemums'.

42. *Animal Farm*
- At the beginning the pigs are on the side of the other animals, opposed to the farmer, and act with them.
- From early on they are seen as leaders – more intelligent than others.
- Old Major's and Snowball's deaths change things. Napoleon is shown as power-hungry.
- Parallels with USSR and other totalitarian regimes.
- Symbolism of pigs walking on their hind feet.
- Final chapter where pigs are indistinguishable from humans and accepted by humans.

43. *Never Let Me Go*
- Kathy tries to understand him, giving us anecdotes about him to try to work out why he behaves as he does.
- He is seen as different from other pupils – an outsider, picked on. His 'tantrums' seem to come from nowhere.
- His conversations with Miss Lucy help him and Kathy to understand more about their situation.
- His relationship with Ruth and Kathy's view of it.
- How he changes as he gets older – what he is like as a donor.
- Kathy's love for him and her feelings after his 'completion'.

44. *Anita and Me*
- She lies to her parents and disobeys them. However, she loves and looks up to both of them.
- She is fascinated by their past lives in India and their love story, seeing it as a love match, not an arranged marriage.
- She idealizes them – the only slight implied criticism is that they are a bit pushy and her mother wants to interfere in people's lives.
- The relationship changes a bit after the birth of her brother, when she does not get as much attention.
- They are seen as different from other parents in the village, because of their culture and their class.

45. *Pigeon English*
- Harri's desire to belong makes him want to join the Dell Farm Crew.
- Harri feels sick when he sees the reality of them attacking an old man.
- Tension between gang culture and the family and community's Christianity. Harri thinks gang members can be brought to God.
- Rules are important in gangs and in family life – gangs as perversion of family.
- Language used to show culture and membership of the group.
- Novel inspired by real-life crime – how this context influences its reception.

46. *The Woman in Black*
- The first chapter takes place many years after the events, establishing his character and his settled family life.
- Kipps decides to write his tale to show what a 'real' ghost story is like.
- His status and profession help to make him a reliable narrator.
- The young Kipps is sceptical about the supernatural but is curious and has a sense of adventure.
- Readers empathize with Kipps and his personal tragedy.

47. *Oranges Are Not the Only Fruit*
- Up to this point Jeanette has been educated at home by her mother.
- References to the Bible, religion and prayer are a feature of their normal conversation.
- Mother is seen doing the usual things a mother might do – making tea, ironing etc. – but this is juxtaposed with images of religion.
- Mother has passed on her zeal and sense of being different to Jeanette.

- The relationship changes when Jeanette discovers her sexuality and her mother cannot accept it.
- At the end there is a sense that this relationship has made Jeanette and remains the most important in her life.

Questions 48–56
48. Look at the mark scheme on page 135 (for pages 104–105 Practice Questions). Your answer might include:
- Who is in danger and from what? – 'Exposure', 'Bayonet Charge', 'Remains', 'Poppies'.
- Soldiers put in danger by those above them – 'Bayonet Charge', 'Exposure'.
- The brigade seen as one – other poems focus on individual reactions.
- Rhythm and metre.
- Sense of excitement and bravery – 'Remains'; contrast 'Bayonet Charge', 'Exposure'.
- Use of imagery, literal and figurative.
- Use of language, e.g. alliteration in 'Exposure'.
- Voice/speaker not in danger – 'War Photographer', 'Poppies'; contrast with 'Exposure', 'Remains'.

49. Your answer might include:
- The nature of the parting – here 'sorrow and tears', bitterness in 'Neutral Tones', death in 'Porphyria's Lover'.
- Reasons for the parting – she has broken her vows but the details are not given.
- The use of imagery of nature – 'Neutral Tones'.
- Romantic ideas about love and relationships.
- Direct address to the loved one.
- Feelings of poet/voice towards subject – 'love–hate relationship' or love turning to hate?
- Regular structure with simple rhyme scheme – apparent simplicity expresses deep feelings.

50. Your answer might include:
- Relationship between father and child from father's point of view. 'A Child to his Sick Grandfather' is from a child's point of view; 'My Father Would Not Show Us' and 'One Flesh' are about parents.
- It takes the form of an anecdote written in the first person – 'Neutral Tones', 'The Manhunt'.
- Feelings of wanting to protect the loved one – 'A Child to his Sick Grandfather', 'i wanna be yours'.
- Sense that time cannot be stopped – 'One Flesh', 'My Father Would Not Show Us'.
- Use of the imagery of nature – 'Neutral Tones', 'She Walks in Beauty'. Images taken from war – 'The Manhunt'.
- Structured in four regular quatrains (rhyming *abab*) within a single stanza. Use of iambic pentameter (heartbeat). Regularity controls emotion – Sonnet 43, 'Neutral Tones'.

51. Your answer might include:
- Focus on the effect of war/conflict on a non-combatant, here a mother – 'War Photographer', 'Belfast Confetti', 'What Were They Like?'
- Poem tells the story of a personal experience, using the first person – 'Belfast Confetti', 'Exposure', 'War Photographer'.
- Use of symbolism (dove, poppies).
- Imagery of everyday things to describe emotion/experience – here sewing, in 'Belfast Confetti' writing.
- Sense of the vulnerability of the soldier, here seen as a little boy – 'Exposure'.
- Conversational tone / free verse – 'War Photographer'.

52. Your answer might include:
- A place evokes memories of people and happier times – 'Adlestrop', 'Absence'.
- Personal feelings expressed through a description of place – 'Adlestrop', 'Stewart Island', 'Composed upon Westminster Bridge', 'On Romney Marsh'.
- Sad/melancholy tone – 'To Autumn', 'Stewart Island', 'Absence'.
- Literal imagery reflecting mood / pathetic fallacy.

- Short lines – sense of breathlessness reflecting walk up hill.
- Use of rhyme – irregular patterns / half rhymes.

53. Your answer might include:
- Power in nature / powerful men. The hawk could represent human power as well.
- Use of the first person – voice of the hawk in 'Hawk Roosting'; three voices, within each other, in 'Ozymandias'.
- The hawk's power is in the present and unchallenged / Ozymandias has lost his power.
- Violent images in 'Hawk Roosting' / images of decay and emptiness in 'Ozymandias'.
- The hawk analyses his power and violence in a cool, conversational way.
- Shelley draws lessons about power, while Hughes just presents it.
- In 'Hawk Roosting' the short stanzas and punctuation convey the bird's confidence and sense of command.

54. Your answer might include:
- 'An Arundel Tomb' is about people who have been dead for centuries. 'The Soldier' is about the poet's own death.
- Both poets talk about something physical remaining. In 'The Soldier' it is only dust; in 'An Arundel Tomb' a great monument.
- Larkin's tone is quite melancholy as he considers time passing, whereas Brooke seems enthusiastic and feels sacrifice is worthwhile.
- Larkin does, however, conclude that love survives death – as does Brooke.
- Consider lost love, memories and starting again in 'Love after Love'.
- Bereavement in 'Long Distance II' – different reactions to death.
- The feelings of loss in 'A Broken Appointment' and 'The Sorrow of True Love.'

55. Your answer might include:
- Hardy adopts a persona, giving a voice to the ordinary soldier, while Brooke is writing as himself.
- 'The Man He Killed' suggests that war is futile and had no meaning for the soldier; Brooke does not question the war but gives a sense of pride in his sacrifice.
- While 'The Man He Killed' is about the experience of killing someone, 'The Soldier' is concerned with being killed.
- The language of 'The Man He Killed' is down-to-earth and appropriate to the speaker; the language of 'The Soldier' is self-consciously poetic and rhetorical.
- 'The Man He Killed' has the structure, metre and rhyme scheme of a ballad, giving it an upbeat quality, in spite of the subject. 'The Soldier' is in iambic pentameters, and has a melancholy tone.
- 'Consider the descriptions of battle in 'The Destruction of Sennacherib' or 'Anthem for Doomed Youth.'
- Think about how the poets seek empathy with 'the enemy' in 'Vergissmeinnicht' or 'What Were They Like?'
- Write about poets' ideas about war and nationalism in 'Flag' or 'Partition'.

56. Your answer might include:
- 'Out, Out' tells a story in the third person; 'The Soldier' uses the first person to reflect on the poet's feelings.
- Brooke writes about his own possible death in war, something expected of a soldier. Frost's poem is about a completely unexpected and horrific accident.
- Frost writes in detail about the horror of the event; Brooke is not concerned about what it is like to die, but rather about what his death represents.
- Brooke's two stanzas and iambic pentameter give the poem a controlled, formal feel. Frost's

free verse makes his poem conversational and lacking in control.
- Both have a sense of place but for Brooke England is an idea as much as a place, while for Frost the setting is a beautiful, peaceful backdrop in contrast to the event.
- Brooke sees his death as meaningful / having a purpose, whereas the boy's death in 'Out, Out' is seen as random and pointless, of little importance to others.
- Consider the young poet's reflections on his own death in 'When I have fears that I may cease to be'.
- Think about the narrative style, imagery and the attitude to children in 'Cold Knap Lake' or 'Red Roses'.

Question 57
57. Look at the mark scheme on page 136 (for pages 106–107 Review Questions, Q2), decide which description is closest to your answer and then decide which mark to give yourself.

a) Your answer might include comments on the following:
- Hardy gives a voice to an ordinary soldier.
- Persona's motives for becoming a soldier – poverty, unemployment.
- The ballad form tells a story in a simple, traditional form – appropriate to subject.
- Rhythm and rhyme give it a cheerful tone in contrast with the subject.
- The language is colloquial, the voice working-class.
- His attitude to his enemy – he sees him as the same kind of man.
- Reference to 'traps' places him in the country, perhaps as gamekeeper or a poacher. He is used to killing animals.
- The nature of the deed contrasts with the friendly language.
- Makes a strong point about war through a naive voice who sees his 'foe' as an individual like himself.

b)
- Differing situations – one going to war, the other having returned.
- Past tense / future tense.
- Difference in focus – one on killing, the other on dying.
- Sense of patriotism in 'The Soldier' absent from 'The Man He Killed'.
- One matter-of-fact, the other emotional.
- Use of imagery in 'The Soldier'.
- Difference in tone created by rhythm/metre and language.

Glossary and Index

a

abbreviation   a shortened form of a word or phrase (48)

abstract noun   a noun which names something you cannot touch or feel, such as an idea or emotion (26)

accent   a way of pronouncing words, usually associated with a region or area (86)

act   a division of a play (87)

active voice   when the subject is the person or thing doing: for example, 'the dog bit the boy' (10)

adjective   a word used to describe a noun and add more detail (26)

adverb   a word used to describe verbs, often ending in 'ly', such as 'swiftly', 'anxiously' (26)

alliteration   repetition of a sound at the beginning of two or more words (29, 96)

alphabetical order   the arrangement of information according to the alphabet (A–Z) (31)

ambiguity   when something has more than one meaning (adjective – **ambiguous**) (83, 94)

anecdote   a short account of an interesting or humorous story, often used to reinforce a point being made (49)

antagonist   the person who opposes the protagonist (40)

apostrophe (')   punctuation mark used to show possession or omission (9)

archaic   old-fashioned, no longer in use (97)

argument   a reasoned point of view (49)

article   a short piece of writing, usually in a newspaper or magazine (46)

aside   a line or lines addressed to the audience while other actors are on stage (61)

associate   connect mentally (7)

assonance   repetition of a vowel sound within words (29, 96)

atmosphere   the tone or mood of the text (39)

attitude   a writer's feelings or opinions about something (94)

audience   a group of people who hear, watch or read something (48)

authorial voice   the writer speaking directly to the reader (71)

authority   power or influence, often because of knowledge or expertise (adjective – **authoritative**) (57, 75)

autobiographical   describes writing about the author's own experiences (46)

autobiography   the story of the author's life (45)

b

ballad   a form of poetry which tells a story, usually in quatrains with a regular metre and rhyme scheme (92)

Bildungsroman   a novel that tells the story of someone growing up (72)

biography   the story of someone's life (45)

blank verse   poetry which has a regular metre but does not rhyme (99)

blog   a diary or journal published on the internet (short for weblog; **blogger** – a person who writes a blog) (31)

broadsheet   a 'serious' newspaper, so-called because they used to be published on large sheets of paper (50)

bullet point   a typographical symbol used to introduce an item in a list (31)

c

caesura   a pause in a line of poetry, sometimes denoted by a punctuation mark (62)

chapter   a division within a book (31)

character   a fictional person (38)

chronological order   order of time, starting with the earliest event (31)

clause   a phrase (group of words) which could stand alone as a sentence, having a main verb (10)

climax   the dramatic high point of a story, usually at the end (37)

colloquial   conversational or chatty (noun – **colloquialism**) (75)

colon (:)   a punctuation mark used to introduce a list or an explanation (8)

comma (,)   a punctuation mark used to separate clauses or items in a list (8)

complex sentence   a sentence containing more than one clause (but not a compound sentence) (11)

compound sentence   a sentence consisting of two clauses of equal importance, joined by a conjunction (10)

conceit   an elaborate or far-fetched simile or (extended) metaphor (63)

conclusion   end (30)

concrete noun   a noun that names something you can touch or feel (also **common noun**) (26)

conjunction   a word used to join two words, clauses or phrases and show the relationship between them: for example, 'and', 'but', 'because' (10, 27)

connective   any word or phrase used to join phrases, sentences or paragraphs (13)

connotation   a meaning that is suggested by the use of a word or phrase (28)

consonant   any letter that is not a vowel (6)

content   subject matter; what something contains (22)

context   circumstances (56)

contraction   making two words into one by leaving out letters and using an apostrophe: for example, 'doesn't', 'I'm', 'who's' (6)

counter-argument   an argument that answers one that has already been given (49)

court   the people surrounding a king or queen (57)

d

deduction   working something out or coming to a conclusion (69)

determiner   a short word that comes before a noun and helps to define it, including the definite article ('the') and indefinite article ('a') (27)

diagram   a plan, sketch, drawing, or outline designed to demonstrate or explain how something works (82)

dialect   words or phrases particular to a region (14)

dialogue   speech between two or more people; conversation (59, 87)

diarist   a person who writes a diary (44)

diction   the choice of words and phrases used (26)

difference   a way in which two or more things are not alike (22)

direct address   speaking directly to the audience, usually using 'you' (49)

direct speech   the actual words spoken, put in inverted commas (41)

director   a person who directs plays (83)

discourse marker   a word or phrase that connects sentences or paragraphs (13, 49)

divine right   the idea that the right to rule comes from God (57)

dramatic monologue   a long poem in which a fictional character speaks to a reader or an audience (92)

e

ellipsis (…)   punctuation indicating that something has been left out (9)

embed   with reference to a quotation, to place it within sentences so that the whole sentence makes sense (24)

emotive language   language used to provoke emotions, such as shock or pity, in readers (28)

end-stopping   ending a line of verse with a punctuation mark (also called lineation) (98)

enjambment   when lines are not end-stopped but the sense runs on between lines or even stanzas (98)

evidence   information referred to in order to support a point being made (20)

exclamation mark (!)   a punctuation mark used to denote extreme emotion (8)

explicit   open, obvious (18)

exposition   setting the scene or giving background information at the beginning of a story (36)

extended metaphor   a series of similar metaphors combining to create one image (63)

f

fable   a story, often about animals, that gives a moral lesson (81)

feature   a newspaper or magazine article that is not a news report (46)

figurative imagery   the use of an image of one thing to tell us about another (39)

form   a type of writing or the way it is presented (44)

formal language   language that is similar to Standard English and used in situations where it is not appropriate to be too conversational (75)

fragment   another word for a 'minor sentence', one which does not contain a main verb (10)

free verse   poetry that does not have a regular metre or rhyme scheme (99)

full stop (.)   a punctuation mark that marks the end of a sentence (8)

function   what something is used for (73)

g

genre   a kind or type of literature: for example, detective story or romance (44)

grammar   the study or rules of how words relate to each other (14)

h

headline   heading at the top of a newspaper or magazine article (50)

homophone   a word that sounds the same as another word but is spelled differently and has a different meaning (6)

hyperbole   exaggeration (adjective – **hyperbolic**) (28, 49)

i

iambic pentameter   a line of poetry consisting of ten syllables with the stress on every second syllable (62)

identify   select; name (18)

image   a picture, also used metaphorically of 'word pictures' (59, 84)

imagery   when words are so descriptive that they paint a picture in your mind. Imagery is used to allow the reader to empathize or imagine the moment being described. (29, 42)

imply   to suggest something that is not expressly stated (noun – **implication**; adjective – **implicit**) (20)

inciting incident   an event that starts the action of a story (36)

indent   to start writing a little way in from the margin: for example, to start a new paragraph (12)

indirect speech   speech that is reported rather than quoted: for example, He said that she was there (41)

infer   to deduce something that is not openly stated (noun – **inference**) (20)

informal language   conversational language that is spoken between people who are usually familiar with one another (44)

interpret   when you infer meaning and explain what you have inferred, you are interpreting implicit information or ideas (noun – **interpretation**) (20, 83)

interval   a break during a performance (87)

intrusive narrator   a narrator who is outside the action but comments on it (37)

inverted commas (' ')   punctuation marks used to indicate quotations, titles etc. (9)

irony   when words are used to imply an opposite meaning, or sarcastic language that can be used to mock or convey scorn (adjective – **ironic**) (75)

isolate   separate; place apart (7)

issue   a subject being discussed (59, 71)

j

journal   a form of diary (44)

journalism   writing in a newspaper or magazine (46)

l

literal imagery   the use of description to convey mood or atmosphere (39)

location   place (81)

lyric   a short poem about feelings (93)

m

medium   means of communication (plural – **media**) (83)

metaphor   an image created by directly comparing one thing to another, such as 'my brother is a little monkey' (29, 97)

metre   the pattern of stressed and unstressed syllables in poetry (62, 99)

minor sentence   a 'sentence' that does not contain a verb – also known as a 'fragment' (10)

mnemonic   a way of remembering information, especially spellings (7)

modal verb   a verb that shows the mood or state of another verb: for example, 'could', 'might' (14)

mood   the general feeling conveyed (see **atmosphere**) (39)

morality   ideas of good and bad behaviour, or right and wrong (57)

motif   an idea or image that is repeated at intervals in a text (71)

motivation   the reason(s) for doing something (60)

movement   a group of writers who share similar ideas about literature and/or write in a similar style (92)

musical theatre   a form of drama including music (81)

n

naive narrator   a narrator who does not understand what is going on, often a child (72, 85)

narrative   story (37, 40)

narrator   the person telling a story (37)

non-fiction text   a text that is mainly based on facts and not made up (44)

noun   a naming word (10, 26)

o

object   (in grammar) the thing or person to whom something is done (in the active voice) (10)

octave   a set of eight lines of verse (98)

omission   missing out (9)

omniscient narrator   a narrator who is outside the action and knows everything (37, 85)

onomatopoeia   the use of a word that sounds like what it describes (29, 96)

opening   start, beginning (30)

opinion   what someone thinks (18)

oxymoron   two contradictory words placed together: for example, 'bitter sweet' (63)

p

paragraph   a section of a piece of prose writing, shown by indentation or leaving a line (12, 31)

parallel phrasing   repeating the structure and some of the words, phrases, clauses or sentences (43)

paraphrase   to put something in your own words (24)

parenthesis   brackets; a word or phrase inserted into a sentence to explain something (plural – **parentheses**) (9)

passive voice   where the subject has the action done to him or her: for example, 'the boy was bitten by the dog' (10)

past continuous tense   the tense used to convey an action that continued for some time in the past, e.g. 'he was talking for hours' (15)

past perfect tense   the tense used to describe events that happened before those being described in the past tense, using 'had' (15)

past tense   the tense used to described something that has happened (7)

pathetic fallacy   either a form of personification, giving nature human qualities, or using a description of the surroundings to reflect the mood of a character (29)

perfect tense   a form of the past tense, using 'has' or 'have' (15)

period   an amount of time (80)

persona   a fictional voice used by a poet (95, 96)

personal pronoun   a pronoun that stands in for the names of people (14)

personification   when an inanimate object or idea is given human qualities (29)

perspective   point of view (44, 71)

Petrarchan or Italian sonnet   a form of sonnet consisting of an octave and a sestet (98)

playwright   a person who writes plays (85)

plot   the main events of a story (59)

plural   more than one (6, 14)

possession   belonging or ownership (9)

preposition   a short word showing the relationship of one thing to another: for example, 'to', 'under' (10, 27)

present tense   the tense used to describe things happening now (15)

pronoun   a short word which replaces a noun ('I', 'you', 'he', 'she' etc.) (26)

proper noun   a noun that names an individual person or thing, such as a place or day, and has a capital letter (26)

prose   any writing that is not poetry (62, 83)

protagonist   the main character, the person whom the story is about (37, 40)

psychology   the study of the human mind (69)

pun   word play, when words are organized in an amusing way to suggest other meaning (50)

q

quatrain   a set of four lines of verse (98)

question mark (?)   a punctuation mark used at the end of a question (8)

quotation   words or phrases taken directly from the text (verb – **quote**) (24)

quotation marks   inverted commas when used around a quotation (9)

r

recipient   the person who receives something, especially a letter (45)

refer   mention or allude to something (noun - **reference**) (24)

refrain   a repeated line or lines, usually at the end of stanzas, in poetry (96)

register   the form of language used in particular circumstances (26)

relative pronoun   a word such as 'who', 'which' or 'that', used to connect clauses (11)

repetition   when words, phrases, ideas or sentences are used more than once – this can be used to highlight key issues and make important sections more memorable (28)

report   an account of something that has happened, often in a newspaper (46)

reported speech   see **indirect speech** (41)

reverse chronological order   ordering events by putting the most recent first and working backwards (31)

review   an article that gives an opinion on, for example, a film, play or book (46)

rhetoric   the art of speaking (adjective – **rhetorical**) (28)

rhetorical device   a language technique used to influence an audience (49)

rhetorical question   a question that does not require an answer, used to make the reader think about the possible answer and involve them in the text (28)

rhyme   the use of words with the same endings to make patterns (98)

rhyming couplet   two successive lines of poetry that rhyme (62, 98)

rhythm   the beat of the writing, usually in poetry (99)

s

scene   a division of a play, often within an act (87)

script   the text of a play (83)

semantic field   the area from which words and phrases have been taken (26)

semi-colon (;)   punctuation mark used to connect clauses, also used in lists (8)

sentiment   feeling (69)

sestet   a set of six lines of verse (98)

setting   where and when the action takes place (39, 71)

Shakespearean or English sonnet   a form of sonnet popularized by Shakespeare, consisting of four quatrains and a rhyming couplet (98)

sibilance   repetition of 's' sounds (29)

significance   what something means or stands for (73)

silent letter   a letter within a word which is not pronounced (7)

similarity   a way in which two or more things are alike (22)

simile   a comparison of one thing to another using the words 'like' or 'as', such as 'the raindrops fell like tears' (29, 97)

simple past tense   the form of the past tense usually formed by adding '-ed' (15)

simple sentence   a sentence that only contains a main clause (10)

singular   one (14)

skim read   to read quickly in order to find something in the text (22)

slang   informal language, often local and changing quickly (14)

social order   where people are 'placed' in society, with some more important than others (57)

soliloquy   a speech to the audience, expressing a character's thoughts or feelings (plural **soliloquies**) (61)

sonnet   a form of poetry, usually a love poem, of 14 lines (63)

source   the origin of something, used by examiners to describe texts used in exams (47)

speech marks   inverted commas when used around direct speech (9)

Standard English   the variety of English generally accepted as the correct form for writing and formal speech (14)

stanza   a section of a poem, often called a verse (31, 98)

strapline   a subheading under a headline, which explains or expands on the headline (50)

stress   (in poetry) emphasis (99)

subheading   used to break up the text and guide the reader through various sections (50)

subject   the person or thing that a sentence is about (10)

subordinate clause   a clause that contains extra information (11)

summarize   give a shortened account of something, retaining the meaning (noun – **summary**) (22)

supernatural   not belonging to the natural world; magical (69)

syllable   a unit of pronunciation (99)

symbol   an object that represents something else: for example, an idea or emotion (adjective – **symbolic**) (29, 75, 97)

synthesis   the combining of two or more things (verb – **synthesize**) (22)

t

tabloid   a type of newspaper, less serious and easier to read than a broadsheet, traditionally in a smaller format (50)

terminology   use of appropriate, often specialized, words (101)

text box   a box which contains text (31)

theme   subject matter: what the text is about rather than what happens in it (58)

third person   he, she, it (singular); they (plural) (15)

tone   the overall feel or attitude of the writing (74)

topic sentence   a sentence, usually the first in the paragraph, which tells you what the paragraph is about (12)

turning point   an event that changes the direction of a story (37, 87)

u

unreliable narrator   a narrator who cannot always be trusted (85)

v

verb   a doing, thinking, feeling or being word (7, 26)

verse   poetry (62)

viewpoint   point of view (83)

vocabulary   words used (26)

voice   the narrator or speaker; his or her characteristic style (41, 95)

volta   a turn or change in a poem, especially between the octave and sestet in a Petrarchan sonnet (98)

vowel   a, e, i, o, u (6)